# AUGUSTINE
## (BIG HYSTERIA)

Contemporary Theatre Studies

A series of books edited by Franc Chamberlain, Nene College,
Northampton, UK

**Please see the back of this book for other titles in the Contemporary Theatre
Studies series.**

# AUGUSTINE
## (BIG HYSTERIA)

by
## Anna Furse
with a
Foreword
by
Elaine Showalter

**harwood academic publishers**

Australia • Canada • China • France • Germany • India
Japan • Luxembourg • Malaysia • The Netherlands • Russia
Singapore • Switzerland • Thailand • United Kingdom

Published in the Netherlands by Harwood Academic Publishers.

Amsteldijk 166
1st Floor
1079 LH Amsterdam
The Netherlands

---

**British Library Cataloguing in Publication Data**

Furse, Anna
  Augustine: (big hysteria). – (Contemporary theatre studies;
  v. 20)
  1. English drama – 20th century
  I. Title
  822.9'14

  ISBN 3-7186-5936-0 (softcover)

Application for permission to perform *Augustine* (*Big Hysteria*) must be made to Anna Furse, c/o Jacqueline Korn, David Higham Associates Ltd., 5–8 Lower John Street, Golden Square, London W1R 4HA, England.

Cover photograph: Augustine undergoing an attack (*Tétanisme*).

For Jack

# CONTENTS

# INTRODUCTION TO THE SERIES

*Contemporary Theatre Studies* is a book series of special interest to everyone involved in theatre. It consists of monographs on influential figures, studies of movements and ideas in theatre, as well as primary material consisting of theatre-related documents, performing editions of plays in English, and English translations of plays from various vital theatre traditions worldwide.

Franc Chamberlain

# ACKNOWLEDGEMENTS

The author wishes to thank the following:
Annie Castledine
Anne and Chloe Kilcoyne
Ariane Koek
Veronique Leroux-Hugon
Shona Morris
Marcia Pointon
Elaine Showalter
and Robert Robertson

# LIST OF PLATES

(Between pages 14 and 15)

1. Augustine undergoing an attack (*Attitudes Passionnelles*).
2. Augustine undergoing an attack (*Tétanisme*).
3. Augustine undergoing an attack (*Attitudes Passionnelles*).
4. Shona Morris as Augustine in Anna Furse's original production 1991.

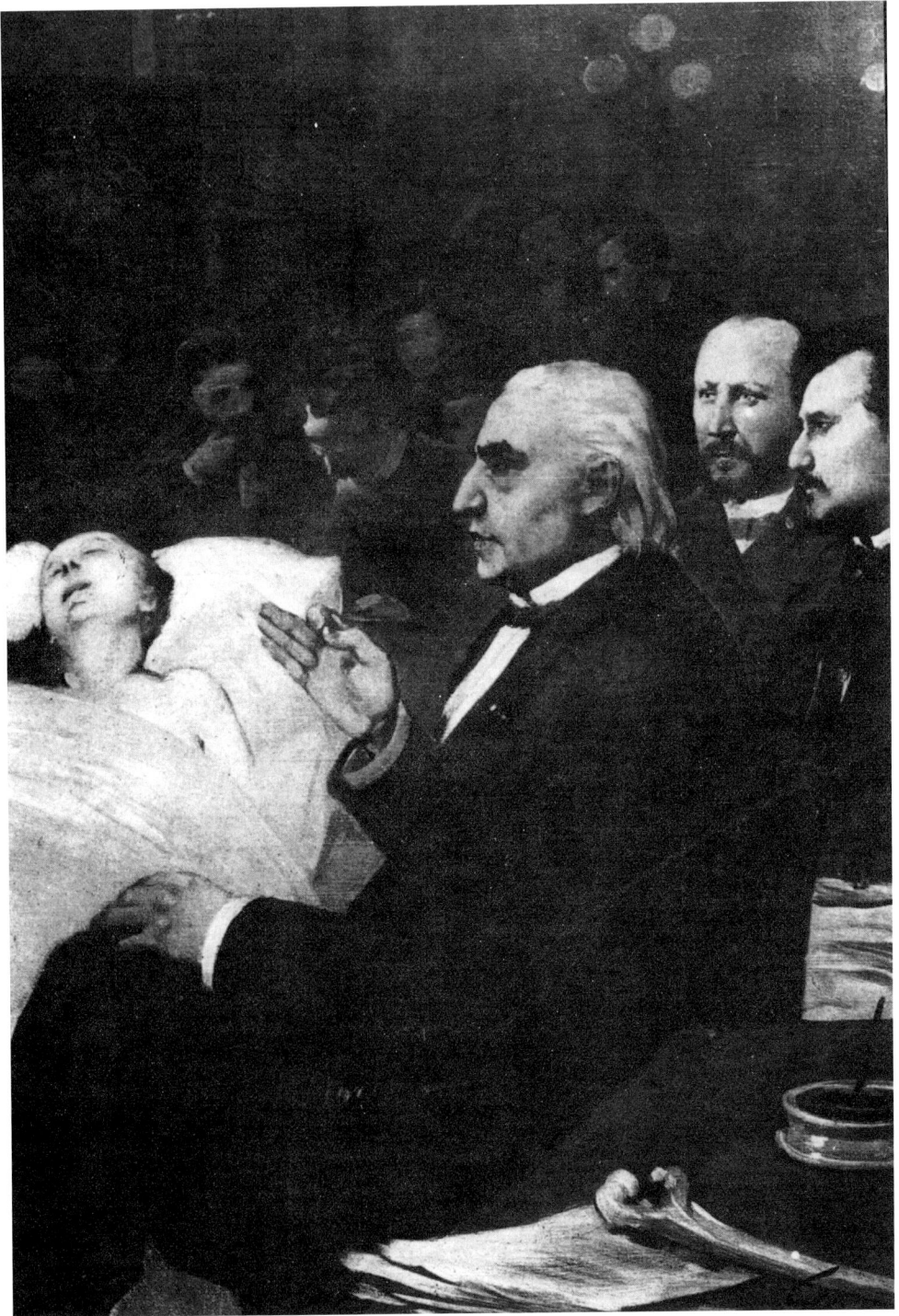

Charcot teaching. Photo: courtesy of S.I.P.A. Presse

# FOREWORD

*Augustine* (*Big Hysteria*) by Anna Furse, first produced in Plymouth in 1991, is one of the most important plays in the new feminist theatre of hysteria. Like Hélène Cixous's *Portrait de Dora* and Terry Johnson's *Hysteria*, *Augustine* draws on the history of psychiatry to produce an innovative performance that is also a critique of the psychoanalytic appropriation of women. Hysteria and theatre have a centuries-old connection. On one hand, metaphors of the histrionic have long been part of the medical discussion of hysterical women. In the nineteenth century it was commonplace medical wisdom that hysterics, as one French doctor noted, were "veritable actresses," who "know no greater pleasure than to deceive." On the other hand, the classical theatre, from *Medea* to *Hedda Gabler* to *The Crucible*, has acheived some of its greatest effects through the representation of female hysteria.

*Augustine* is set in the greatest hysterical theatre of all: the Paris clinic of Professor Jean-Martin Charcot. From 1882 to the year of his death in 1893, Charcot was the impresario of a group of hysterical women who became known as the stars, queens and divas. In his amphitheatre at the Salpêtrière, Charcot gave public lecture-demonstrations of hysteria attended by writers like Turgenev, the Goncourt brothers, Maupassant, Nordau and Gustave LeBon; by artists, intellectuals, dandies and actresses like Sarah Bernhardt; and by cabaret performers like Jane Avril. Not until Jacques Lacan's lectures at St. Anne's Hospital a century later drew crowds of up to a thousand intellectuals, journalists and tourists would there be a similar phenomenon.

A dominating figure with a piercing gaze, often called the Caesar, or Napoleon, of hysteria, Charcot labelled, interpreted and recorded a systematic lexicon of hysterical gesture, a veritable alphabet, grammar and syntax of body language. Arguing that hysteria was an organic disease with a clear and consistent set of symptoms in both women and men, Charcot set out to demonstrate that the dramatic seizures of *grande hystérie* could be induced or stopped by hypnosis, allowing doctors to examine its stages and determine its "laws". Using the Salpêtrière's fully-equipped photographic atelier, Albert Londe recorded the poses of hysterical women patients and published them in the asylum's annual *Iconographie*. Called "grande" hysteria to distinguish it from the minor headaches and banal complaints of "petite" hysteria, the seizures in

Charcot's clinic moved from visual disturbances to sensations of choking, to athletic contortions, and then to the famous *attitudes passionnelles*, the most theatrical poses of the performance. Charcot gave them significant titles: *appel, supplication amoureuse, moquerie, menace, érotisme*, and *extase*. As Jan Goldstein has described them, the *attitudes passionnelles* were "vivid physical representations of one or more emotional states, such as terror, hatred, love; the patient, endowed with an actress's agility in the second period, was now said to display the talents of a mime or dramatic actress." We cannot doubt that the *attitudes passionnelles* were cultural constructs, organized and indirectly taught within the asylum itself, and reinforced by all the pictorial representations resembling poses from the French classical theatre.

Among Charcot's hysterical divas, Augustine was the most extensively photographed. She had been brought to the hospital in 1875, when she was fifteen years old. Her hysterical attacks had begun at the age of thirteen, when she was raped by her employer, a man who was also her mother's lover. Intelligent, coquettish, pretty and quick, Augustine was an apt apprentice of the hysterical theatre. Among her gifts was her ability to time and divide her hysterical performances into scenes, acts and intermissions, and to perform on cue with the click of the camera.

But Augustine's apparent docility took its toll on her psyche. Doctors paid no attention to her accounts of her nightmares, nor listened to her story of abuse. During the period when she was being repeatedly photographed, she began to see everything in black and white. In 1880, she began to rebel against the hospital regime; she had outbreaks of violence in which she tore her clothes and shattered windows. In June, doctors gave up on her case and confined her to a locked cell. But Augustine was able to use on her own behalf the histrionic abilities she had learned at the clinic. Disguising herself as a man, she managed to make a successful escape from the Salpêtrière.

Freud studied with Charcot in 1886, and was deeply impressed by his ideas and his energy. But Freud would develop his own treatment for hysterical women – a talking cure, which involved listening as well as looking and recording. In the play, Anna Furse takes poetic licence in bringing Augustine, Charcot and Freud together in the asylum as Freud begins to *listen* to hysterics and to interpret their gestures as a private body theatre of the unconscious. In this poetic and powerful drama, we see the hysterical woman, the male voyeur, the male listener – a triangle that would become paradigmatic in the psychiatric history of women. As Hélène Cixous has written, "the hysteric, whose body is transformed into a theatre for forgotten scenes ... does not write. ... But the master is there. He is one who stays on permanently. He publishes writings." The publication of *Augustine* helps restore the woman's voice to the record.

*Elaine Showalter*

# INTRODUCTION

## The Theatre for Forgotten Scenes

*"They accuse us of madness – but can there be any better way of going into hiding than to become the mechanism itself and so really not have anything to do with what creates us or with what we are bound to measure".*
Ursula Margozta Benka: "A Convent of Schizophrenic Nuns" [1]

*Augustine* (*Big Hysteria*) is based on the true case history of Augustine surviving in records at The Salpêtrière Hospital in Paris. I first came across this extraordinary story in Elaine Showalter's excellent *The Female Malady*. [2] Her account of this bizarre "Grande Hystérique" struck a deep and nagging chord: Augustine, star of the Salpêtrière Hospital in the 1870s, favourite of neurologist Professor Jean-Martin Charcot, was treated to intensive photorecording till she became colour-blind, finally escaping from the hospital dressed as a man. A grainy photograph in Showalter's book shows her apparently posing, a beatific Giselle on her bed, hair loose, nightgown slipping, arms raised ecstatically heavenwards. Someone had titled it: *Supplication Amoureuse* (Amorous Supplication). Who? And who was this hysteric-showgirl? Why the theatricality of her incarceration? How on earth did she escape and in whose clothes? I was impelled to seek further. Armed with a commission from Annie Casteldine (then Artistic Director of Derby Playhouse) I went to Paris to begin my research at the Salpêtrière which survives today as a major neurological hospital. Its library is named after Charcot and in the corner of his beloved oak-carved bookcases, were three musty volumes of the *Iconographie Photographie de la Salpêtrière*. [3] These are unique publications, illustrated with faded sepia photographs for which there are no negatives. Hysteric case histories sketched, snapped and

---

[1] Benka, Margaret, "A Convent of Schizophrenic Nuns" in *The Edinburgh Review* (1978).
[2] Showalter, Elaine. *The Female Malady: Women, Madness and English Culture*. Virago Press (1987).
[3] Bourneville and Regnard, *Iconographie photographique de la Salpêtrière*. Vols 1–3. (Paris 1878).

scribbled down. I discovered Augustine, the most recurring presence of all, tableau upon tableau of her balletic histrionics: Augustine in nightgown, in maid's uniform, exploded with bright lights into a sudden statue of shock, or rigid as a board stretched between two chairs like some conjuror's levitationee. Then there were the *Attitudes Passionnelles* (Postures of Passion) as Charcot called them – little crazed billetsdoux, psychological gestures of erotic role-play with an invisible lover.

All this in the presence of the hospital photographer's gaze, and the implication of that gaze. The role of the spectator has influenced the posing and Augustine is aware of, indeed manufacturing, the message being communicated. She is quite literally *making a spectacle of herself* for reasons the play attempts to unravel. We must also remember that this visual documentation took *minutes* to register on a plate and was a far more cumbersome process than our own instant-snapping.

The archiving isn't only pictorial. The *Iconographies* also record many of Augustine's utterances during attacks and provoked by drugs such as ether or amyl nitrate (to which she herself despairingly refers). How fast did these scribes write? Handwriting is far slower than the battery-fire of hysteric babble. Did they take poetic licence, or were her speeches so recurrent in theme and content that it was easy to keep track? Such ardent archivists! What industry! And all this commissioned by Professor Charcot himself. As Director of the Salpêtrière, he established these 19th century recording studios at the hospital in an effort to wrench his profession away from age-old superstition and prove, with all this elaborate evidence, a pathology of hysteria beyond the congenital, the hereditary and the organic. In short, and I shall return to this later, Charcot was beginning to prove hysteria was *in the patient's mind:*

*"It all goes back to remembering".*
Freud [4]

According to the *Iconographies* Augustine was the child of domestic servants, farmed out to relatives until the age of six, from which time she spent seven years in a convent. Evidently a bright, rebellious and precocious child, she was deeply traumatised by severe punishment administered to her by priests and nuns – "the slammer" as she herself called it and, on occasion, exorcism by dousing in ice-cold water. Augustine was suspected of being possessed by the Devil, then a common diagnosis of unmanageable Catholic girls. (It is worth noting here that Charcot was to become obsessed with the connections he first sighted between hysteria and demonic possession, using his vast

[4] Freud, Sigmund and Breuer, Joseph. The Pelican Freud Library Volume 3: *Studies in Hysteria*. Penguin Books (1978).

knowledge of classical art for this and publishing in 1886 a fascinating study of his research in *La Démoniaque dans l'art* (*Demonic Possession in Art*).[5] This research had far-reaching implications:

> "*Charcot's widely publicized contribution to the hysteria diagnosis, which increased dramatically during his tenure as hospital director, were for him and his followers a way of attacking demonic possession and religious ecstacy, and of getting institutional control of hospitals and schools taken away from the Catholic Church. That is, Charcot's work on hysteria contributed to an anti-clerical campaign promoting the triumph of positivism*".
>
> Dianne Hunter: "Representing Mad Contradictoriness in Dr. Charcot's Hysteria Shows"[6]

At the age of 13, Augustine's mother placed her in the household of a Monsieur C where she herself lived as housekeeper. (In my play this person is named Carnot so as to imply possible transference by Augustine between her abuser and her doctor (Charcot). In the same vein I take the liberty of calling Augustine "Dubois" (literally "from the woods") as a sign of her embodiment of Nature. Interestingly, the Salpêtrière Hospital uses several names and letter codes for Augustine: she features in records also as Louise, X, A and L – a significant arbitrariness: the lack of standardisation in naming her suggests the observer-scribes and their seniors found no fixed-point of identity in the young patient. Any stability she may have had was thus subverted by mere language. So this performs yet another insult to the Augustine-self, who was thus merely *playing the parts* (quite literally) ascribed to her.)

Monsieur C and Augustine's mother struck a deal: Augustine would learn appropriate female domestic skills in service whilst having the privilege of learning to read and write alongside Monsieur C's own children. None the less, the teenager had to sleep in cubby-hole under the stairs. Augustine was soon to learn that her special status in this household was doubtless due to the fact that her mother was Monsieur C's mistress and that he had designs on the young girl himself. Monsieur C raped Augustine at knife-point whilst she was still only 13. He continued to sexually abuse her, possibly with her mother's knowledge and consent. Augustine, terrified lest he carry out his threat to kill her, soon developed classic hysteric symptoms: recurring visions (especially of eyes – Monsieur C had used his eyes to control Augustine both during and after rapes), numbness, pains in her abdomen, great fits during which she exhibited uncontrollable energy, suffered sensations of suffocation,

---

[5] Charcot, Jean-Martin and Richer, Paul. *La Démoniaque dans l'art*. Éditions Macula (1984).
[6] Hunter, Dianne. "Representing Mad Contradictoriness in Doctor Charcot's Hysteria Shows" in *Madness and Drama*. Cambridge University Press.

then finally hallucinations and hysterical babble, paralysis of one half of the body and garish nightmares. Two years later her mother delivered her daughter to Charcot's renowned clinic at the Salpêtrière Hospital where she remained for six years.

Professor Charcot presided over this huge women's asylum which he ghoulishly called "our living museum of suffering". He specialised in hysteria and hypnosis – the latter a fashionable phenomenon in Europe pioneered by the work of the 18th century Austrian physician Mesmer (from which the word "mesmerise" derives) which was to make such a profound contribution to the founding of psychoanalysis by Freud in the latter part of the 19th century. Charcot instantly diagnosed Augustine a classic "Grande Hystérique" and, during her incarceration under his charismatic tutelage, elevated her to a kinky kind of star-status in his famous public lecture-demonstrations *Les Leons de Mardi* (The Tuesday Lessons). Whilst she was regularly paraded in front of gazing crowds of medics and laypeople at the Charcot freak-shows, Augustine's medical records attest to recurring behavioural leitmotifs: nightmares of *blood, fire, revolution, theatre* and *escape* (sic). As if these weren't clues enough, she acted out regular mini-escapes, sorties into the hospital gardens at night in the rain. Also, and this is crucial, she cyclically recounted her rapes. Augustine's imagery returns, explodes and mutates like shamanistic incantation: fear of eyes, *"snakes in your trousers"* which she insists must be got rid of, and *"rats in my bottom"* or *"tummy"*. Was Augustine a classic Freudian symbolist before even he had located his theories on the matter? One could hardly find more potent language by which to describe the penis and anal and vaginal penetration:

> *"What do you know about medicine? (...) I don't want you anywhere near me! (...) I won't uncross my legs (...) Oh! You've hurt me too much... no you won't be able to! (...) Help! (...) Bastard! Nurd! Jerk! (...) I'm sorry! I'm sorry Monsieur! Let me go! (...) It's impossible! (...) You don't want any more? Again! (...) Take that snake out of your trousers! (...) You wanted me to sin before you, but you'd already sinned (...)"* (she opens her mouth, puts her hand in as though to take something out of it) *"I'm confiding secrets to you (...) Spoken words fly away, written ones remain (...) You're pulling my leg! You can say Yes all you like, I'm saying No! (...) I won't uncross my legs (...) It's impossible! (...) I don't have time... (bis) ... the rats are in my bottom! Get rid of them!...".*
>
> *Iconographie photographique de la Salpêtrière*[7]

---

[7] *Iconographie photographique de la Salpêtrière*. Volume 2.

Important incidents during this time included: firstly, two visits to the Salpêtrière demonstrations by Monsieur C. Not surprisingly, she reacted to her rapist's perverse voyeurism with extreme attacks. Secondly, the loss of her sense of colour (loss of sight and hearing prevail today as well-known hysterical symptoms). This is Augustine's particularly significant message: *She takes on the qualities by which she is described by others.* She not only *is* a black and white photograph but she incorporates the very idea: her whole world becomes transformed into monochrome. Where she is pacified, she becomes *actively* passive. She celebrates her pariah status like a drag queen on a Saturday night. She goes further into an idea than was ever intended. She is a supreme dramatist ever busy interpreting her own condition. Her art is self-parody. One is reminded of Sartre's anatomy of Jean Genet's marginal status:

> *"In his very depths, Genet is first an object – and an object to others... . One can expect that Genet, who is an object par excellence, will make himself an object in sexual relations and that this eroticism will bear a resemblance to feminine eroticism" ... "He had to make himself become the Other that he already was for Others".*
>
> Jean-Paul Sartre: *Saint Genet*[8]

Augustine doesn't lose her sense of colour because she is *mad* but because she is merely *embodying* that which Others (her medical voyeurs) condemn her to. She is "writing her body" with characteristic theatricality. Her body is saying: *I am a photograph. But I am also a camera and I see you out there in black and white.* This is part of the complex language of signs and gestures that are her strategy for both declaring her suffering and protecting herself from the male world which threatens her even as it claims to heal.

At her worst, Augustine might undergo 200 attacks a week, be straitjacketed (often at her own request), or locked in padded cell. Meanwhile, the omni-present doctors' fingers were on stand by to probe her vagina for signs of sexual arousal during such attacks. Her hospital notes diligently record "abundant discharge" alongside recordings of temperature, spasms, micturition and menstruation.

> *"I would like to interrogate this compromise and this menace, when, as regards hysteria, a doctor can hardly avoid witnessing as an Artist the georgeous pain of a body in the throes of its symptoms... . It is the problem of the violence of the gaze in all its scientific pretensions".*
>
> Georges Didi-Huberman: *L'Invention de l'hystérie*[9]

---

[8] J.-P. Sartre: *Saint Genet – Actor and Martyr*. A Plume Book from The New American Library (1963).
[9] Didi-Huberman, Georges. *L'Invention de l'hystérie*. Éditions Macula (1982).

Treatment? This included amyl nitrate, ether, gold (administered internally and externally), morphine, and the speciality of the house – an equestrian-looking contraption called the Ovarian Compressor. This object, consisting of a kind of tourniquet to the ovaries by means of a drumstick-like object being pressed tightly into them, was designed to somehow either induce or abate an attack according to the doctor's desired effect. Unsurprisingly, the ovaries of sexually abused teenagers were exceptionally sensitive to touch. Thus Charcot was also able to achieve similar results by exerting pressure on the ovary with the palm of his hand. Hypnosis, Charcot's forte, was also regularly employed. With a patient under hypnosis, he was able to prove his central thesis and most significant contribution to the understanding of the neuroses as opposed to the psychoses: *hysteria has no organic base*! This was simply demonstrated by removing or moving the patient's hysterical paralysis which he could easily achieve once they were under his spell. So, the womb was not capable of acrobatically jumping round the body – an ancient misconception still fashionable in the 19th century and which is the etymological root of the word *hysteria*. These women were feigning their symptoms. The paralysis and seizures were masquerades! The body was lying! But why?

> *"He who has eyes to see and ears to hear becomes convinced that mortals can keep no secret. If their lips are silent, they gossip with their fingertips: betrayal forces its way through every pore"*.
>
> Freud [10]

Far from dismissing this psycho-physical play-acting, the *grands gestes* and histrionic dances of hysteric contortions, Charcot enthusiastically studied them to examine the powers of mind over matter. The connection he was unable or perhaps disinterested in making, was the link between traumatic experience and neurosis. This was to prove Freud's advance and the foundation of psychoanalysis. To Charcot Augustine's utterances were *"much ado about nothing"* (sic). He was a self-professed *"visuel"* (seer/man of vision). He offered Augustine his persistent, piercing and intransitive gaze, and with it held her in thrall. Charcot was not so interested in cure as in categorisation. His obsessive visual archiving of such patients as Augustine was a search for an archetype, for classic symptoms, for the pathology of hysteria rather than a demonstration of any interest in the individual root causes indicated by the patient's specific history. He was a man with new technology at his fingertips, and he used it with relish. Where Freud excavated the

---

[10] Freud (ibid).

patient's mind in private, Charcot scanned her body in public. Charcot looked, Freud listened.

*"Beauty will be convulsive"*.
André Breton [11]

Meanwhile, whether or not The "Charcoterie" listened, Augustine still babbled her verbal lava-flow all over the amphitheatre and onto the page as she convulsed and stretched, twisted and leapt in her telling tarantella:

> *"The hysteric, whose body is transformed into a theatre for forgotten scenes, relives the past, bearing witness to a lost childhood that survives in suffering. (...) for the hysteric does not write, does not produce, does nothing – nothing other than making things circulate without inscribing them. The result: the clandestine sorceress was burned by the thousands; the deceitful and triumphant hysteric has disappeared. But the master is there. He is the one who stays on permanently. He publishes writings"*.
> Hélène Cixous [12]

Augustine was the perfect archetype of hysteria, with star-status in Charcot's medical freakshow. Her audience would consist of (male) doctors – Les leçons de Vendredi (Friday Lessons) or "le tout Paris" at the famous Leçons de Mardi. Records reveal the Goncourt Brothers and Victor Hugo among the many luminaries to witness this revolutionary spectacle of suffering compliantly provided by such young and disturbed women. Interestingly, Sarah Bernhardt was herself a regular audience member:

> *" 'After the first words of her vibrant, lovely voice I felt I had known her for years' recorded Sigmund Freud, who went to see her play on every possible occasion during his visits to Paris (where he was studying with the great Charcot at the Salpêtrière: he might well have seen Sarah at Charcot's weekly open lectures, which she attended regularly, eager for the clues they might offer regarding human behaviour in extremis"*.
> Jules Lemaître, quoted by Ruth Brandon in *Being Divine* [13]

According to Brandon, "The Divine Sarah" none the less experienced feelings of *"distaste, almost fear"* (ibid) from this research. One suspects this wasn't the general audience response. The Tuesday Lessons evoke Bedlam a century earlier, where a paying public would goggle at the deranged as a form of entertainment. Like all stars, Augustine was the

---

[11] André Breton, *Minotaure*, no. 5, 1934.
[12] Cixous, Hélène. *The Newly Born Woman*. Manchester University Press (1987).
[13] Brandon, Ruth. *Being Divine – A Biography of Sarah Bernhardt*. Secker and Warburg (1991).

object of a fetishistic voyeurism. Her doctors sketched her, sculpted her, photographed her, notated her, pressed her, probed her, measured her bodily secretions, and then photographed her some more. She cheerfully complied, performing on cue both to camera and audience, exploding at touch and dramatising scenarios at the slightest hypnotic suggestion. In short, Augustine had *it*. But this *it*, like some of Hollywood's more famous victims after her, was born of her powerlessness in a patriarchy. Augustine's stardom stemmed from an abreaction to a childhood rape trauma. Unable to cry for help, silenced by the threatening eyes of her rapist and by 19th-century propriety as regards feminine utterance, she converted her distress into physical symptoms – *"inscribing the body"* as Cixous calls it. She literally em-bodies pain. The drama she enacts through her own muscular tissue is quixotic, a mercurial set of clues accompanied by verbal pyrotechnics rich with obscenity. Sexual revelation tumbles from her breathless "clownisms" and *"attitudes passionnelles"*.

> *"I'm confiding secrets to you... Spoken words fly away, written ones remain... You're pulling my leg! You can say Yes all you like, I'm saying No!... I won't uncross my legs... It's impossible! I don't have time... I don't have time".* [14]

It is Augustine-the-actress-shaman who signals psychic pain through physical transformation, the mind-over-matter phenomenon of her body's eloquence, which impelled me to take poetic licence and include the young Freud in my play. He is a sleuthing device. With his presence, a more contemporary psychoanalytical narrative becomes possible. Freud and Augustine actually missed each other at the Salpêtrière by a decade, although he would certainly have studied similar cases there. Freud's experience under the "Napoleon of Neuroses" and the "Cçsar of the Salpêtrière", as Charcot was dubbed, was to prove seminal. Rivetted by his teacher's use of hypnosis on hysterics, the young Freud was subsequently to open his own private practice in Vienna two years later where he hypnotised young hysterics (clumsily apparently). Freud had for some time been in correspondence with an older colleague who was doing pioneering research in hysteria, Joseph Breuer. Freud was soon to shift his technique to Breuer's experiment of "talking therapy" developed with the latter's patient "Anna O" in the early 1880s. With this new technique the patient's stream of consciousness, probed by the attentive ear of the doctor, became the subject of investigation. Psychoanalysis was born. Freud would work well into the next century on his excavations of the "buried cities" of his neurotic patients. In the

---

[14] *Iconographie* (ibid).

play I use an imaginary encounter with Augustine as a catalyst for his shift from a study of the body to a study of the mind. The minds of his Viennese woman patients were (like Augustine) full of sexual traumas, revelations of childhood rape, sexual abuse and incest. Initially Freud believed what he heard but years later was to dismiss these as the expression of latent repressed desire. His Oedipus Theory, developed in the late 1890s as a result of his self-analysis, managed to return our abused hysterics to the status of fantasists and tall-tale-tellers. In *Augustine* (*Big Hysteria*) I collapse Freud's volte-face to imagine it happening in response to a period of interaction with Augustine. Thus during their fictional relationship at the hospital he shifts from ally to disbeliever, from nervous and remote observer to the classic shrink's position sitting at the head of her bed, note-taking as his detached but tenacious interrogations provoke Augustine to her ultimate act of liberation: literal escape and transformation – into drag and off the stage.

> *"I had a lively interchange of opinions with Professor Charcot (both by word of mouth and in writing) on the points of view arising from our investigations".*

Freud [15]

With the inclusion of Freud in the piece, a potent triangle began to take shape as I wrote. This triangle offered a constant dialectic: a shifting balance of power and allegiances between Charcot "the Seer", Freud "the Listener" and Augustine the "Narrator", an actress telling a story the patriarchy chooses to ignore, a subversive protesting at her oppression and converting enforced silence into an eloquent physical text:

> *"In the body of the hysteric, male and female, lies the feminine protest against the law of the father".*

Juliet Mitchell [16]

In terms of language and gender, in the process of writing the play four layers of text began to emerge: Charcot's academic lectures (masculine theory); arguments between Charcot and Freud (masculine debate); dialogues between Freud and Augustine (masculine/feminine dialogue); Augustine's monologues – hysterical, liberational, incantational and confessional (feminine narrative). So, four different languages. The first is one of scientific authority, shot through with a bravura born of confident gallic iconoclasm. Charcot is the official storyteller, the Master of Ceremonies, the charismatic boss. The second: a language of polite

---

[15] Freud, Sigmund. *Report from my Studies in Paris and Berlin, March* 1888. The Pelican Freud Library.

[16] Mitchell, Juliet. *Psychoanalysis and Feminism.* Pelican Books (1974).

and restrained horn-locking, the (Oedipal) struggle between the young Freud and the elder Charcot, pupil to teacher, son to father, and a struggle for ownership of both the *site* and the *idea* of Augustine. The third: a language of shrink to analysand, of adult to child, of man to woman and thus a dialogue of opposites, e.g. scientific enquiry versus flirtation, the formal versus the intuitive. The last: a language of exposure and of celebration, the *"upside down festival"* of which Cixous speaks, the spilling of words as a means of liberation, of reclaiming territory. Such unboundaried utterance is also a rebellion against (patriarchal) Civilisation and a return to a savage (feminine) Nature. In finding these languages and splicing them with imagery, I discovered the need for an *alter ego* for Augustine. I wanted her to have a *doppelgänger* who observes herself and could express pure pre-lingual emotion and her nervous condition. This is the Violinist who must pluck, scream and synthesise emotions through the nerve-gut of her instrument. Taking this idea further, the Violinist offers other important references: at one moment in the play, both Augustines let their nightgowns fall off their shoulders and reveal the F-stops of the famous Man Ray photograph on their backs. This is meant to signify not only how Augustine has become an "instrument of science", callously played by others, but also refers to the Surrealists' appropriation of hysteria in their peculiar use of female psychic disorder in their aesthetic. In 1928 Louis Aragon and André Breton published a 50th anniversary tribute to Hysteria, not surprisingly featuring Augustine's story in words and photographs, provoking unabashed arousal from these subversive Messieurs who breathlessly proclaim:

> *"We surrealists are anxious to celebrate here the quinquagenary of hysteria, the greatest poetic discovery of the end of the nineteenth century, and to celebrate it at the very time when the dismemberment of the concept of hysteria would seem to be an accomplished fact. We who like nothing so much as youthful hysterics – the perfect example of which is furnished by observations relating to the delightful X. L. (Augustine) who entered the Salpêtrière Asylum for Women during Charcot's term on 21 October 1875...(...) Does Freud, who owes so much to Charcot, remember the time – confirmed by the survivors – when interns at the Salpêtrière confused their professional duties and their taste for love?...*
>
> *Hysteria is not a pathological phenomenon and can be considered in every respect a supreme means of expression".*
>
> André Breton and Louis Aragon[17]

---

[17] Aragon, Louis and Breton, André. "The Quinquagenary of Hysteria (1878–1928)" in *La Révolution surréaliste*, no. 11, March 1928.

The suggestion that Freud might have "confused his professional duties" is provocative. I chose to incorporate this idea in imagining the young Freud, a 28-year-old (by all accounts virgin) on a long engagement to his future wife Martha Bernays, too much of a "gent" (and too repressed himself) to admit any attraction to Augustine but nonetheless spellbound by her charms. Meanwhile she, using the only powerful tool at her disposal – feminine wiles – becomes his capricious first client. He listens and learns. She speaks and seduces. They bond against the common father-figure of Charcot. A kind of love-affair, certainly, but one in which they finally betray each other. He abandons her in his pursuit of becoming a Freudian, and she responds by escaping:

> "The child who is vulnerable to sexual abuse is often engaged in a search for love and protection they haven't received elsewhere. This need may then be exploited by an unscrupulous adult, and the child will tolerate the abuse in exchange for the brief illusion of affection it affords. If such a child is eventually lucky enough to have treatment with a psycho-therapist, for the first time he or she meets a person who understands these needs without exploiting them. Understanding is, in fact, the therapist's form of love".
>
> Caroline Garland, Psychoanalyst [18]

My play is set in the late 19th century, however, when asylum patients had only recently been unchained. Augustine remains exploited by her doctors, not only in the most obvious way by Charcot, but also by Freud's ambition and drive (which she teasingly confronts). Freud is fascinated by this young woman's every nuance because she is the site of his début excavation. He is lead by his head, and she, with the unerring instinct of a child, goes straight to his heart, disarming him momentarily as she does so. In fact, the closer to his sexual organs she gets, the more cerebral he becomes. When Augustine finally erupts into her terrible tarantella in the rain she is inventing her own putrid "festival". She declares herself a carnival of smells, juices and rage. She boils over into self-celebratory incantation and finally *enters herself* to take possession of her own destiny.

The play is intended to mimic sessions on the analyst's couch. Sometimes these may uncover huge arcs of coherent information and at others leave the disturbing material of memory a tenuous and fragmented reach away from full consciousness. The audience is deliberately placed in the role of voyeur. They are cast in the role of audience to Charcot's lectures, whilst he, as Master of Ceremonies, treats them as intelligent and concerned. But it is the character of Augustine who

---

[18] Garland, Caroline. Quoted in programme notes to première production of *Augustine* (*Big Hysteria*) (1991).

jostles to be the central narrator and should gradually implicate the real-life audience in their gazing. She sheds clues which they must work out. She comes out and touches them, she counterpoints the mainstream narrative with her own story, she makes the audience work for her. In the end when she springs onto the stage dressed as a battered Vesta Tilley she is literally wearing Freud and Charcot's clothes. These two, stripped of sartorial masculinity, their uniforms of power and authority, sit vulnerable as babies as she delivers her epilogue. It is important that this final entrance brings garish technicolour lighting on stage as a sudden contrast from previous monochrome. This is because Augustine has repossessed herself. Celebrating the recovery of her sense of colour signifies her new and hard-won integrity, her shamanistic re-membering after dis-membering. She has refused to submit anymore, but she isn't even angry. The enemy have been neutralised. She quits their stage and leaves her hysteric career behind her.

*"From the symptoms, then, the stories spill out and spread: the clandestine biographies, our female narratives of disease. The 'Phallocentric Performing Theatre' with its spectacular exorcisms faces closure, now that the foreign body has become our own, now that the flesh, turning its back on its audience, makes words..."*.

Alison Fell[19]

Augustine turns her back on her audience, complete, independent and armed with a disguise of her own conscious making. Her step into this unknown may not herald a bright future (after all what could she have made of her life with all that behind her?) but at least it will be an authentic one.

*Anna Furse*

## Additional Reading
1. Charcot, Jean-Martin. *L'Hystérie*. Privat (1971).
2. Furse, Anna. "Big Hysteria" in *Plays and Players* (June 1991).
3. Gay, Peter. *Freud – A Life for Our Time*. Macmillan Papermac (1988).
4. Gilman, S., King, H., Porter, R., Rousseau, G. and Showalter, E. *Hysteria Beyond Freud*. University of California Press (1993).
5. Goetz, Christopher. *Charcot the Clinician – The Tuesday Lessons*. Raven Press.
6. Jones, Ernest. *The Life and Work of Sigmund Freud*. Pelican Books (1964).
7. Lubimoff, A. *Le Professeur Charcot*. Bibliotèque Publique d'Information, Beaubourg, Paris.

[19] Fell, Alison. Introduction to *Serious Hysterics*. Serpent's Tail (1992).

8. Musée de l'Assistance Publique. *La Leon de Charcot*. Exhibition Catalogue (1986).
9. Owen, A.R.G *Hysteria, Hypnosis and Healing – The Work of J.-M. Charcot*. Dennis Dobson (1971).
10. Roberts, Michèle. *In The Red Kitchen*. Methuen (1990).
11. Zanuso, Billa. *The Young Freud*. Basil Blackwell (1986).

**Useful Addresses**

Archive Photographs from: C.M.T. Assistance Publique, 8 rue des Fosses St Marcel, 75005 Paris, France. Agents: S.I.P.A. Presse, 101 Boulevard Murat, 75016 Paris, France. Tel: (33)1 47 4347 75.

The Salpêtrière Hospital: Hospice de la Salpêptrière, Boulevard de l'Hôpital, 75013 Paris, France. Tel: (33)1 42 16 0000.

The Freud Museum, 20 Maresfield Gardens, London NW3.

**Notes on Staging**

*Language* In many ways this play is about language. Who owns it? Who suppresses it? Who converts it? Who re-invents it? The language is not only verbal but physical and visual. The text is littered with verbal and visual clues which are mostly symbolic-Freudian. For instance, the pin Charcot uses to test Augustine's mock-stigmata is plucked from a scarlet heart-shaped pincushion proferred by Freud. This is an intentional pun on the Catholic bleeding heart (remember Augustine was a convent girl) as well as an image of how carelessly doctors played with her feelings (Freud has this 'heart on his sleeve'). Polyphony (e.g. Augustine's voice doubling with Freud's in the revolution dream sequence) and visual dialectics are devices to create more complex layers of meaning and should be played quite naturally, even when "dancing" such as the men's cigar-rolling sequence when Augustine is performing her contortions and seizures on the other side of the stage. The "dances" are made up of natural gestures in the cigar-dance, or the study of authentic Augustine photographs for her movement. Similarily the long slow dance she performs at the beginning of the play must be based in authentic material. As for her hysteric attacks, they can and should be reconstructed from available archive material.

Because we are dealing here with the language of psychoanalysis, it is possible and desirable for endless overlapping, eavesdropping and shadowing. This relates to all the characters, particularily though with Freud who should be a ubiquitous brooding witness, on-stage as much as possible. This device can also apply to the Violinist, i.e., even when she isn't actually playing, we can observe her observing her Self (the actress).

*Design*   Visually, the piece should not be staged naturalistically but find an appropriate playing space. If possible, slides of the authentic photographs should be projected where indicated.

*Music*   The piece has been written with a strong sense of musical presence. This should both underscore the text and be an event in itself. Sound effects are important to the meanings, e.g. heavy rain (purgation), heavy metal doors slamming (incarceration), argument between the metronome (classical control) and the violin (the soul).

NB. The play should run without an interval.

## Notes on the Original Production

*Augustine* (*Big Hysteria*) was first staged at the Drum Theatre, Plymouth Theatre Royal, on 19 April 1991 in a co-production with Paines Plough for which Anna Furse was then Artistic Director. The Play was originally commissioned by Annie Castledine at Derby Playhouse. The original production toured the UK and the Ukraine in 1991/2. The play has since been published and produced by the Maly Divadlo Theatre in the Czech Republic in 1994 and produced in Copenhagen 1996. A specially commissioned Television extract was screened on Channel 4 in 1994.

The original cast and company were:

| | |
|---|---|
| *Augustine* | Shona Morris |
| *Charcot* | Wolfe Morris |
| *Freud* | James Dreyfus |
| *Violinist* | Anne Wood |
| *Direction* | Anna Furse |
| *Design* | Sally Jacobs |
| *Music* | Graeme Miller |
| *Lighting* | Ace McCarron |
| *Slide Design* | Steve Littman |
| *Production Management* | Nick Ferguson |
| *Deputy Stage Manager* | Sarah Cox |
| *Assistant Stage Manager* | Jerry Donaldson |
| *Press Officer* | Chris Taylor |
| *Photographs* | Hugo Glendenning |

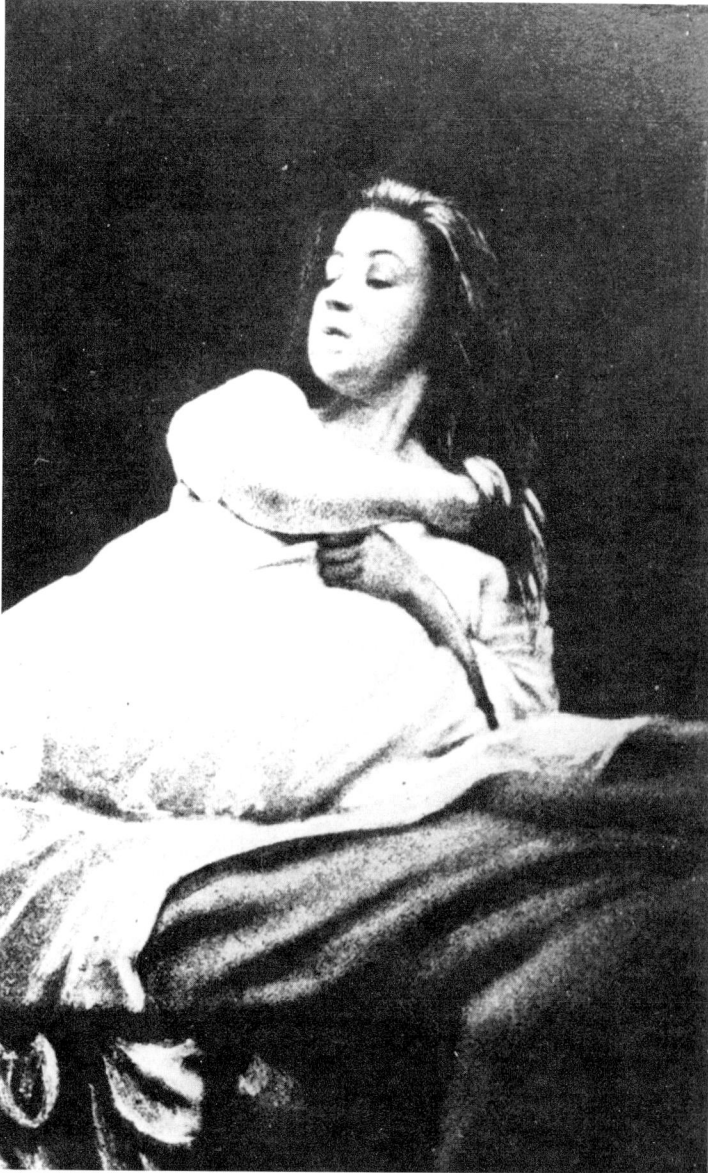

Planche XVIII.

## ATTITUDES PASSIONNELLES

1. Augustine undergoing an attack (*Attitudes Passionnelles*).
Photo: courtesy of S.I.P.A. Presse

Planche XVI.

## TETANISME

2. Augustine undergoing an attack (*Tétanisme*).
Photo: courtesy of S.I.P.A. Presse

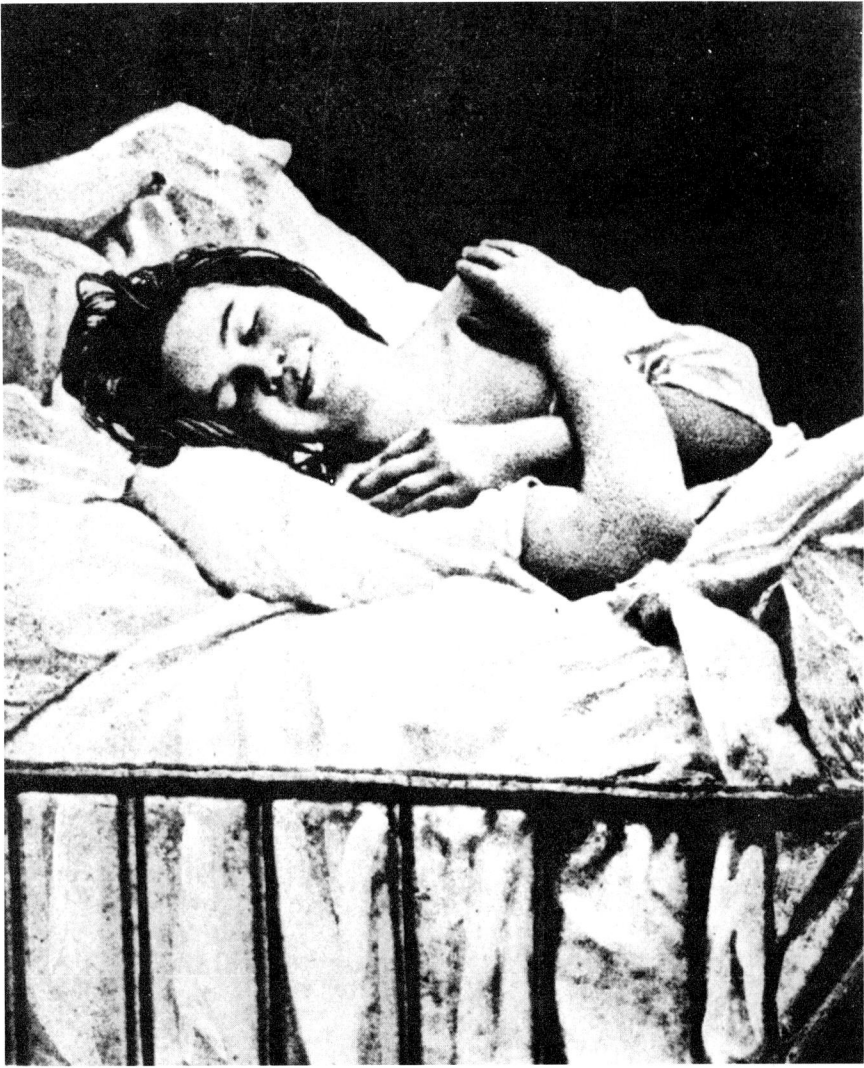

Planche XXI.

# ATTITUDES PASSIONNELLES

EROTISME

3. Augustine undergoing an attack (*Attitudes Passionnelles*).
Photo: courtesy of S.I.P.A. Presse

4. Shona Morris as Augustine in Anna Furse's original production, 1991.

# AUGUSTINE (BIG HYSTERIA)

*The hysteric, whose body is transformed into a theatre for forgotten scenes, relives the past, bearing witness to a lost childhood that survives in suffering... For the hysteric does not write, does not produce, does nothing – nothing other than making things circulate without inscribing them. The result: the clandestine sorceress was burned by the thousands; the deceitful and triumphant hysteric has disappeared. But the master is there. He is the one who stays on permanently. He publishes writings.*

Hélène Cixous (La Jeune Née)

*I want to attempt a terrific feminine. The cry of claims, of trampled down rebellion, of steeled anguish at war.*

*The lamentation of an opened abyss, as it were; the wounded earth cries out and voices are raised, deep as the bottomless pit, these are the depths of the abyss crying out.*

*Neuter. FEMININE. Masculine.*

Antonin Artaud (Seraphin's Theatre)

*It all goes back to remembering...*

Sigmund Freud

*The real AUGUSTINE was admitted to the Salpêtrière in October 1875 and escaped, dressed as a man, on 9 September 1880. All her clinical records end here and nobody knows what happened to her.*

*FREUD spent six months at the Salpêtrière, as a young neuropathologist, on a travel bursary from October 1885 to March 1886.*

*I have chosen to imagine an overlap between AUGUSTINE and FREUD both under the influence of CHARCOT. It was CHARCOT's work on hysteria and hypnosis which had a decisive influence on FREUD's career. Within a year of returning to Vienna, he began to use hypnosis in his private practice. Psychoanalysis was born.*

*All the clinical data in the play is, to the best of my knowledge, accurate. It derives from medical records at the Charcot library in Paris. This includes AUGUSTINE's case history, and CHARCOT's lectures on hysteria as well as his hypnosis demonstrations. AUGUSTINE's utterance, or at least some of it, survives at the Hospital Library and I have used her voice sometimes verbatim but mostly fictionalised.*

*The photographs used in the production can be obtained via the Salpêtrière Hospital.*

A.F.

## CHARACTERS

AUGUSTINE
: *A young woman 15–20 years old. Long dark hair. A child-woman. Part of her extremely advanced for her age and time, the other in suspended childhood.*

THE VIOLINIST
: *Her double.*

PROFESSOR JEAN-MARTIN CHARCOT
: *Late 50s/early 60s. Distinguished-looking: high forehead, strong dark features, thick set eyebrows, prominent nose. Silvery hair down to his collar, swept off his face. Witty, arrogant, eccentric, brilliant. A charming showman who breeds both love and contempt around him.*

THE YOUNG FREUD
: *Bearded. Scholarly. Nervous. Ambitious. In some conflict about his feelings for Charcot, e.g. awe and jealousy. Gives off a sense of preoccupation, of some private scheming at work in his mind. Heavy cough and runny nose from cigars and cocaine.*

*THE ACTION TAKES PLACE AT THE SALPÊTRIÈRE HOSPITAL IN PARIS DURING THE EARLY 1880s.*

*The audience enter to a subtle, almost subliminal soundtrack; a mix of violin, laughter and chatter, pepperings of applause, the sound of a woman crying, rainfall. The whole soundscape should enter and leave the audiences's consciousness like sounds brought on a wind, ghostly gusts. Gloomy light. Moonlight through a large window. Pale walls. A single institutional hospital bed of the late 19th century: an iron four-poster with calico white curtaining hanging from it. This creates a kind of booth, a small mobile stage, and, as now, a screen for slide projections. At this time, projected onto the bed-screen is the photo of Augustine in her 'normal state': her head resting on her right hand, she is a gentle-looking girl, still with puppy fat, her hair pulled off her face and coiled, a buttoned dark dress with white collar and bow at the neck. She is the picture of demure, compliant femininity. Only her eyes, which look out at us, betray both intelligence and pain. They do not smile with her mouth. (NB. THIS WILL BE A DOCUMENTARY PHOTOGRAPH AS WILL ALL OTHERS IN THE PLAY.)*

*As the houselights fade, all lights on stage darken except for the slide image which thus glows stronger. The soundtrack is now a girl child's voice singing, falteringly, the tune of a German children's song:*

> Ach, du liebe Augustine, Augustine, Augustine,
> Ach, du liebe Augustine, alles ist hin.
> Oh, ma belle Augustine, Augustine, Augustine,
> Oh, ma belle Augustine, tout est cassé.
> Oh, my pretty Augustine, Augustine, Augustine,
> Oh, my pretty Augustine, everything's cracked.
> Eyes are cracked, head is cracked,
> hand is cracked, heart is cracked,
> Oh, my pretty Augustine, everything's cracked.

*The effect of this tune is haunting, desolate. By the end of the first verse, the bed and the image projected on it begins to shake violently. The sounds of the actress causing this begin to scream out, throttled gasps to yells and finally to speech. This is accompanied by a live, but as yet invisible VIOLINIST playing.*

AUGUSTINE: Oh, there's something pulling my fingers, pulling my tongue, there's something in my throat... MAMAN!!!!!!!! (*She weeps.*) My neck, oh, my neck, my neck hurts, I can't, can't breathe... MAMAN!!!!

*Slide image and voice cut suddenly. We are momentarily drowned by a burst of applause and laughter on a soundtrack as lights cut to 'amphitheatre': where we discover PROFESSOR CHARCOT, in a state of animation, merry, bouncing on his heels. He is in the middle of a lecture. Acknowledging the laughter he has provoked, he addresses us as if we were his audience at the Hospital. Paternal familiarity and great oratorial charm. He is enjoying his effect on his audience and the opportunity to prove something before them:*

CHARCOT: Let me answer your question, Monsieur, by way of a poetic metaphor for this... asylum... this citta dolorosa of 5000. Our living museum of suffering, was as you may know, at the time of Louis XIII, a saltpetre store. Hence "La Salpêtrière". Now, saltpetre, Messieurs, makes gunpowder, and gunpowder makes explosions. (*He acts out a big explosion with his arms.*) So in this... arsenal of women... with their earth-shattering energies, I, and my colleagues, are simply seeking to defuse our human powder kegs. Your question also raises the issue of whether or not hysteria is an incurable mystery. Now all diseases come from Nature and Nature is most certainly Divine. Severe cold, heat, wet, the restlessness of winds, all play their part in weakening the human body. There's no need to ascribe a special divinity to one disease over another. Each has a nature, power and intrigue of its own;

none is hopeless or incapable of treatment, HYSTERIA INCLUDED! But firstly, WHAT IS HYSTERIA? We must begin by exploring the territory of the hysterical body, then, like cartographers, we must chart it, map out its contours, possess its enigmas...

*A doctor (FREUD) has brought AUGUSTINE in to the amphitheatre. He stands solicitously near her, a nervous, shy young intern. She is in an absolutely 'normal' state, dressed in the same dress as in her portrait photograph. She looks at CHARCOT and at the audience with interest, and a sense of willingness to be there, 'on stage'.*

CHARCOT: HYSTERIA... HYSTERO... WOMB!

*He moves his hand generally over AUGUSTINE's womb area, like a TV weather-reporter. She watches his hand near her body, fascinated.*

Until most recently we doctors thought the womb to be a dancer, or an animal, crouching, leaping round the body and trying to strangle the hysteric by getting stuck in her throat. So sneezing was prescribed as a cure for hysterical attacks, and even labour pains! (*A very French handgesture – 'bof'.*) This of course is nonsense! The UTERUS IS NOT AN ACROBAT! No, we must seek answers elsewhere. So, if I use methods which may seem to belong more to the fields of art and literature, to the poet rather than the scientist, let me simply say this: I am a visionary! Mine is a SCIENCE of looking (and I know those artists amongst you, will vouch for the deep revelations the mind's eye can bring forth); art has as its basis, observation, experience, and reasoning. My method is a form of vivisection if you like – and these slices of life conjure answers BEFORE MY VERY EYES! And I repeat, nothing, but nothing is incurable... Not even this apparently elusive disease, subject of my Tuesday Lessons. In a moment, I will make pain palpable to you. I'll make you recognise all its characteristics. I set before you a case of Grande Hystérie! Time will tell if she will be a Classic example! Doctor?!

*Turns to AUGUSTINE. Looks intently at her.*

FREUD: Mile Augustine Dubois, Professeur.
CHARCOT: Thank you. So, Messieurs... by way of demonstrating my own empirical methods, you will now witness a typical diagnostic encounter between myself and a new patient about whom I know nothing ... yet!

*CHARCOT stares at AUGUSTINE for a very long time. He walks around her as though she were a sculpture. He pats his fingers on his lips, breathes loudly and occasionally blows out through his fingers. She watches him, curious. She watches him watching her. She is aware of the audience and 'performs' this encounter for them. She is almost amused by him, although as the silence continues she bites her lip, impatient for this scrutiny to end. This too she signals to the audience. It does, abruptly with a question from behind her which makes her jump.*

CHARCOT: How old are you?
AUGUSTINE: 15 and a half years, Monsieur le Professeur.

*CHARCOT nods to audience, as though he expected this answer. Reads from notes handed to him by FREUD.*

CHARCOT: *Mother, 41 years, domestic servant, in good health, Father, 45 years, sober... seven children, the eldest being Louise – Augustine – born at full term, breastfed till nine months, sent to relatives in Bordeaux until the age of 6(1/2). From 6(1/2) to 13 was with nuns in Ferté-sous-Jouarre. There she was put "in the slammer", because she got bored of reading* The Lives of Saints *in the refectory. Sometimes, the sisters would administer corporal punishment, slaps...*
AUGUSTINE: Oh I often deserved it...
CHARCOT: *(A bit surprised at her interruption.) She has a bright, capricious, wilful disposition and is too outspoken for her age. She is intelligent. Has learnt to read, write and sew. Works as a laundrymaid in the same household where her mother is housekeeper... to a certain Monsieur Carnot and family...*

*At the mention of her mother and Monsieur Carnot AUGUSTINE has visibly tensed, a fact which escapes the attention of CHARCOT but not FREUD.*

CHARCOT: *The mother, who brought her to us, has no idea what has caused her daughter's illness, which started 2 years ago. Says that A always felt her attacks coming (pains in the left side of the stomach) gentle at first, culminating in leaps on the bed, screaming. No foaming at the mouth and no involuntary urination.*

*AUGUSTINE is embarassed by this but deals with it by setting a sweet smile on her face and fixing her gaze directly ahead.*

CHARCOT: *Finally, last April, a series of attacks leaving her with a paralysis of the right side, couldn't use her right arm nor walk because her right leg folded and gave way. The attacks coincided with the development of breasts and pubic hair... A is a big, well-built girl, with nothing of the ways of the child remaining. She almost has the allure of a fully fledged woman, but has not yet started menstruating.*

*AUGUSTINE is now wearing her smile like a rigid mask. CHARCOT scrutinises her.*

CHARCOT: *Admitted for paralysis and severe hysterical attacks... 21st October 1885.*

*CHARCOT gazes at AUGUSTINE one last time, then gestures for FREUD to take the patient away. During the following, the actress is changing into a hospital gown in the bed-booth.*

CHARCOT: Well, Messieurs, that's all we have time for today. We will, I'm sure, be meeting our young patient again. I am certain she will prove our hypothesis. She will most certainly be susceptible to provocation. Provocation! That is to say, it will be possible, through hypnosis or ovarian compression, to induce the full, classic cycle of Grande Hystérie I am so keen to show you. It is the most picturesque of illnesses... a fascinating phenomenon! That is why I have built here at the hospital such a vast... observatory for recording, and above all defining its form – perfect as a symphony. Here at the Salpêtrière, science and art are bound together. With my illustrators, my sculptors, my photographers, we are a team of witnesses. And, like ancient astronomers, we gaze, and chart all the secrets of the universe. Stars exist. Fact. It is only for us to prove it, discover and name them...

*Lights cut to the 'ward' where AUGUSTINE is having her photograph taken. This effect is achieved by flashes of bright white halogen light from floor level, so that each 'photo' has a ghostly, grainy, and theatrical look about it. We must understand from this how long it takes for a photograph to be taken with the technology of the age. AUGUSTINE is hardly moving a muscle during most of this. She is wearing a white nightgown, long and plain but cut away from her neck. In her hands she is clutching a bundle of coloured ribbons which she keeps running her fingers through, fidgetty. We hear, but still do not see, the VIOLINIST playing something very lyrical during this. Augustine is counting for the flashes out loud.*

AUGUSTINE: Twenty ricketty buckets... twenty-one ricketty buckets, twenty-two ricketty buckets... twenty-three ricketty buckets... twenty-four ricketty buckets... twenty-five... BANG! (etc.)

*Voice and violin cut suddenly to blackout. When lights fade up, Augustine is standing on her bed, her violinist double at a distance with her back to audience. Huge projections of the 'attitudes passionnelles' photographs, whilst Augustine dances the sequence of poses, in slow motion. She smiles throughout, the coquettish charm of a striptease artist converging with the studied control of a ballet dancer: histrionic, erotic, ecstatic. The violinist plays a passionate and rasping counterpoint to Augustine's sweet, lethargic and compliant dance. It ends with both women turning their backs to the audience and taking off their nightrobes. Their backs are tatooed with F stops (cf. Man Ray photograph). Blackout. A slow dawn finds Augustine in bed in the 'ward'.*

*CHARCOT sweeps in, FREUD in tow, looking on with both reverence and a degree of shock at his Maitre's bedside manners.*

CHARCOT: So no attacks in four days?
FREUD: Nothing, Professeur.
CHARCOT: Menstruation?
FREUD: No, Professeur.
CHARCOT: Vaginal secretions?
FREUD: Abundant during attacks, but normalising in between.
CHARCOT: And you have been taking samples daily?
FREUD: Yes, Professeur.
CHARCOT: And no change in contraction or paralysis of the right side?
FREUD: No, Professeur.
CHARCOT: Let's see if she is, as I suspect, ovariform.

*Gently, but firmly he puts his hand on her right ovarian region and presses. She screams out.*

AUGUSTINE: Oh Jesus Maman!!! Please don't touch me there!

*He nods. Floats a bottle under her nose. She calms. He pats her head. Walks round her bed, concentrating on her. She is now in pain. Her hands are twisted in her ribbons.*

CHARCOT: If I were to press harder, I would induce a complete cycle of grande hystérie. Now isn't the time. We have too many patients to see.

*He leads FREUD out through the door. En route:*

CHARCOT: You know Doctor Freud, if there's anything I'd like you to take with you back to Vienna, anything you have learned here, it's this: there is no greater satisfaction than to SEE SOMETHING NEW. That is to say, to recognise novelty or to suddenly see things afresh. There is both great value and great difficulty attached to such vision. Why do you think it is that, in medecine, people only see what they have learnt to see? Hmm? No imagination!! To my mind, it is quite marvellous to state how one is suddenly capable of seeing things – new states of an illness, which are probably as old as the human race.

*AUGUSTINE, a little stoned from the inhalation, has been trying to catch their attention during this. As they reach the door:*

AUGUSTINE: Messieurs! Messieurs! Which is your favourite coloured ribbon?

*CHARCOT ignores her. FREUD turns to her, momentarily torn. They stare at each other, a flicker. But he decides to follow CHARCOT who hasn't noticed and is in full flow. We hear him continue outside so that the following overlaps:*

AUGUSTINE: I like red ones best... red like blood
CHARCOT: At a given moment, the light is such that it hits the least prepared minds... what was hitherto residing in the void starts to LIVE... it is just like discovering a new star in the sky...
AUGUSTINE: (*Abandoned, deflated.*)... and the blue ones second best...

*BLACKOUT. The sound of dawn chorus. Light fades up through bluish to bright. AUGUSTINE peeps out through her curtains. Satisfied no one is about she proceeds to prepare herself and her bed/booth. She combs her hair. Licks her fingers and smooths her eyebrows. Pinches her cheeks to make them pink. Makes her bed meticulously, biting the corners, barracks-style, to stretch the sheet pristine smooth. Then takes her coloured ribbons out from under her pillow and ties bows on to the iron frame, then on to her nightgown. Finally, slips her gown slightly off her shoulders, and lies supine on the stage set she has made of her bed. She mutters throughout the above, to an invisible intimate.*

AUGUSTINE: G'morning! I'm learning to be left-handed! (*Giggles as she supports her paralysed hand, manipulates it, uses teeth to tie bows etc.*) No I haven't told anyone at the Salpêtrière. Maman said they'd cure me. That's why I came here. To get better. Normal! (*She darkens.*) Outside in the courtyard there's avenues of trees, cool green tunnels of leaves. They've even changed the shape of the trees you know. They've cut their branches and trained them to grow together so they're all... flat... intertwined... the branches... and the leaves... twisting and curling into each other, so you can't tell whose branch is whose except when you look at the trunks and they're still separate, standing side by side in neat rows... like us girls... all the beds in long rows... neat and tidy... I could easily escape you know. It's only a wall. And beyond that it's only a street. Just imagine, nothing but a wall keeping me off the streets! (*Does a cameo 'whore look' and giggles.*) Listen, all it'll take is two months without attacks and I'm getting out of here. But it's important that I keep out of trouble. What do you mean? Now don't be jealous. Oh, honestly... but he's... he's just a young doctor. He said he really came to cut up children's brains, on some bursary, but when he found out all the exciting stuff that was happening with us girls, and the Professor's genius, the lectures and stuff, he asked if he could learn all about it, so the Professor said yes. I think the Professor likes him because he's so serious and intense. And anyways he's only here for a bit, like me, then he's going back... to Vienna... where he's got a girl waiting... Martha... they have to wait years 'cos he's got no money yet... I know because he told me, Dr Freud. Yes! He talks to me! So... No!... you've got a filthy mind! Filthy! Anyhow, Professor Charcot says I'm special. He did! He says I am a *chef d'oeuvre*, a perfect sample, an... archetype. He says I am a star. I think some of the other girls are jealous. Which is your favourite colour ribbon? I like the red ones best... the red best and the blue second best... I'm ready now, I'm ready... (*Pause. Afterthought.*) I wonder if it's the same underground, if all their roots are tangled together too?

*She looks at the contraction in her right arm, her wrist and hand twisted round. She strokes it. Lights change suddenly.*

*'Amphitheatre' area. The sound of a heavy clock ticking, loud oppressive stillness. Gentle birdsong outside. FREUD is sitting on a chair downstage, back to audience, pen and notebook ready, tapping his fingers, looking at his watch. AUGUSTINE is humming to herself, playing with ribbons in her hair. She and FREUD are apparently playing an eye-contact avoidance game – their eyes keep meeting and they keep averting them. She is watching him watch her. He is trying to watch her without her noticing. Both of them visibly tense and alter their body language at the sound of CHARCOT'S voice offstage:*

CHARCOT: That's a really fine tapestry. Should hang it where more people get to see it...

*Suddenly CHARCOT bursts through the door, briskly hands his hat, coat and cane to FREUD who dispenses with them, gestures to the audience as though to say 'please don't get up or applaud', rubs his hands together, and commences addressing his public:*

CHARCOT: Messieurs. You see before you a classic example of La Belle Indifférence. Our patient exhibits no outwards signs of awareness of her own illness. Instead, she exhibits, placidity, calm, cheerfulness even.

*AUGUSTINE nods, she is playing the eager accomplice. It is as if she is to play out the role of 'lovely assistant' to a great magician. She awaits her cues. We must understand from her behavior in this scene that time has passed and she has become accustomed to these performances.*

CHARCOT: Our patient is suffering from partial paralysis in the right side. As you will see her lower right arm is in permanent contraction. Would you lift your lower right arm, please?

*AUGUSTINE doesn't/can't. Smiles at audience with a show of 'it's hopeless, it won't lift' written on her face. He holds her arm up.*

CHARCOT: Now would you shut your eyes and hold your right arm with your left one, please?

*She shuts her eyes. Her left arm waves around in the general direction of her right arm.*

AUGUSTINE: I don't know where it is. This is really driving me crazy!! Can I stop now?
CHARCOT: She feels nothing! You may stop now and open your eyes. What do you feel?
AUGUSTINE: Nothing, Monsieur le Professeur.

*CHARCOT takes a large pin from a heart-shaped pincushion proferred by Freud. He pricks Augustine with it as he speaks.*

CHARCOT: And now?
AUGUSTINE: Nothing, Monsieur le Professeur.
CHARCOT: You see, I have pierced the skin... er... slightly... drawn a little blood, and yet there is ABSOLUTELY NO SENSATION! We are reminded of the skins of sorceresses. Prick a stigmata diaboli, there will be no sensation. Sometimes, even, there will be no blood. Indeed the comparison between hysterics and witches is not to be passed over lightly. Scratch an hysteric, find a witch! (*Chuckles. Charcot pricks her again and she doesn't respond. She looks angry, frustrated, yet ever fascinated by the spectacle of her own body in his hands.*) I refer you to my book *The Demonic in Art* for a detailed study... The shamans turn themselves into birds or tigers. Our hysterics turn themselves into numb grotesques. Twisted, paralysed versions of their former selves. And speaking of witches, en passant, consider, gentlemen, the root of the word medecine: from Medea, a witch if ever there was one! So we medeasin men might not be so far off the track after all, eh? (*To Augustine.*) Come now, don't give us your bad temper young lady! Where's your lovely smile, eh?
AUGUSTINE: Honestly he pricks me like a pincushion and I still got to smile!
CHARCOT: Indeed. Now, does this paralysis and lack of sensation have an organic base? Answer: hysteria is ignorant of anatomy. Hysteria

produces its own symptoms in exaggerated form. If this young lady's paralysis had an organic basis, her upper arm would also be affected. For it is these muscles which control flexion in the lower arm. But this is not the case.

*He pricks AUGUSTINE's upper arm and she cries out.*

AUGUSTINE: Jesus, Mary, Mother of God and all the saints in heaven!

*He turns away from her. She produces her red ribbons which she winds around her palms with her left arm and her teeth as one would a bandage, awkward but successful.*

CHARCOT: So, what is the root of this symptom? I put before you today that hysteric patients PRODUCE THEIR OWN SYMPTOMS by auto-suggestion. In other words, here before us is a body which is LYING to us. It is manifesting the physiologically impossible! Now, I want to forge a concept of hysteria which doesn't lie. And for those sceptics among you, who accuse us of charletanism, would you kindly acknowledge the courage we experimenters have shown in breaking with all traditions, in defying all fear, and in facing the subject squarely! There are more things in Heaven and earth than are dreamt of in all thy philoso...

*CHARCOT has got quite carried away and been tapping his own palm with the pin. There is blood on his hands. He looks at them, attempts to cover up. FREUD offers him a white handkerchief with which he mops up. This bloodstained object appears to intrigue AUGUSTINE. Suddenly the lights BO into a slide projection drenching the set. Actors suspend. An Eerie atmosphere. AUGUSTINE, hands knotted up in red ribbons, in an urgent whisper and very fast:*

AUGUSTINE: Sister Jeanne said: "Take your hand away, you dirty, dirty girl!" Her face was lit up by the candle. She was dripping hot wax on my pillow, right near my face. Her face was all red and her skin was wobbling on her cheeks. Her eyes were all whites. She said: "God will punish you for this, my child. The flames of hell burn all sinners! The Devil has got into you! You know yourself! You know what we do to little girls who've got the devil in them? You are unclean!" They threw icy water in my face. The next day I was put in the slammer again, my hands tied together. I hate Sister Jeanne. She has hands like a dead person. Green and fat.

*Lights back to normal, scene resumes.*

CHARCOT: And today, Messieurs, some proof. I shall employ the power of hypnosis to INDUCE certain hysterical symptoms. Now, let us not forget, gentlemen, that things of the organism AREN'T as precise as things mechanical. They say that experiments on animals never work as well in public as they do in the lab. Never mind though, if we don't succeed as we wish it, it will be a significant learning exercise nonetheless!... You see, this young lady is admitted to this hospital with partial paralysis on the RIGHT side. In a week, a month, tomorrow, this could easily have moved to the left. The paralysis has no organic base. And if it has no organic base, then the MIND must have played its part!

*During this, CHARCOT mimics the movement of paralysis in his own body. AUGUSTINE looks on spellbound, unwinding her ribbons.*

CHARCOT: Ah the powers of the mind over matter! Ever since antiquity, you can find a series of phenomena which can only be explained by this singular PROVOKED NEUROSIS: the HYPNOTIC STATE!... .

*CHARCOT turns AUGUSTINE's face towards him so they are both profile to the audience. After a while he takes his fingers and places them on her eyelids. She closes her eyes and appears to sleep... he floats a bottle under her nose. She wakes, smiling. CHARCOT looks at audience.*

CHARCOT: Simple lavender water! Our props are inexpensive! Now lift your right arm! (*She does so.*) And now, my dear, go and shake hands with the audience!

*She does so, delighted by her success. Beaming like an actress at curtain call, she shakes hands with members of the audience, thanking them as she does so.*

CHARCOT: Come back now. Sit down.

*He stands behind her. Shuts her eyes. Gets a gong and strikes a fulsome tone. She wakes into a frozen expression – melodramatic – of alarm. Her whole body is engaged. He takes a stick and touches her lower left arm. She instantly goes into the identical seizure she has just lost on the right hand. CHARCOT displays his success to the audience. He takes his stick and starts to 'sculpt' her face into different expressions. He talks as he does so:*

CHARCOT: ... and at all times in Man's history, what is called ascetic contemplation was in fact produced by the prolonged fixation of the gaze on some shiny, brilliant object, upon which some special quality, some saintly power, was attributed.

*He is 'moulding' her body and she is free – associating with the physical cues he gives her, now with gestures. He folds her arms in prayer. AUGUSTINE's whole body becomes suffused with saintliness. Her eyes gaze heavenward.*

CHARCOT: And what do you see?
AUGUSTINE: I see Saint Theresa!

*She is delighted to be in communion with her saint. She whispers to her as though the saint were asking her questions.*

CHARCOT: And what does Saint Theresa do?
AUGUSTINE: She makes me better!
CHARCOT: And how does she make you better?
AUGUSTINE: She's the patron saint!
CHARCOT: The patron saint?
AUGUSTINE: Of headaches!
CHARCOT: Quite so. Now, these contemplations would be swiftly followed by hallucinations, apparitions, and even attacks of ecstasy. In a certain sect in Algeria, these phenomena are most intense. The adepts sit around a fire at night. Gradually, they fall into an ecstatic trance and let out long cries. Some have convulsive fits. The anaesthetic then becomes complete, and they lick red-hot coals, some even swallowing live spiders, and scorpions. Serious accidents can ensue...

*He intercepts her enthralled gaze with his hand. She follows it. He draws a bird shape in the air with his finger. He flies the 'bird' and AUGUSTINE's gaze is transfixed to it. It becomes a kind of* pas de deux, *with him leading her dance. Her face is full of joy. She laughs with pleasure. Suddenly CHARCOT draws a snake on the ground. Her whole body contracts into a huge gesture of terror. He adds the bird back in with his other hand, so he is dancing out a ritual fight between the snake and bird. The bird makes short pecking movements to the snake which is circling and circling. She responds to every physical nuance. Suddenly, he gives her a sheet of white paper.*

CHARCOT: Here are some nice potatoes.
AUGUSTINE: You're trying to bribe me now!

*she takes the paper, gingerly, but starts to eat it.*

CHARCOT: But can't you taste? Those potatoes fell in the dustbin!

*She spits the paper out, retching with disgust, wiping her tongue, etc. CHARCOT gives her his top hat.*

CHARCOT: This is your baby, your dear little baby...

*She rocks the "baby" and sings the tune of "Ach du liebe Augustine" as a lullaby. CHARCOT now advances towards her. She drops the hat, her face contorted in horror. She falls backwards into a faint, caught by FREUD.*

CHARCOT: Where are you?
AUGUSTINE: I don't know.
CHARCOT: Who has caught you falling?
AUGUSTINE: I don't know.
CHARCOT: Who are all those people watching you?
AUGUSTINE: I don't know.
CHARCOT: Who am I?
AUGUSTINE: Professor Jean-Martin Charcot.

*CHARCOT indicates to FREUD to lay her on the bed.*

CHARCOT: And so, Messieurs, proof that the hysteric's mind selects that which she wishes to retain of reality. Our young lady here chose to retain my name, whilst apparently being in a trance-like state. She can do the same with her body. She can choose, quite literally, how to sculpt it. (*He taps his forehead.*) The IDEA of movement IS movement; the idea of absence of movement IS motor-paralysis. The production of paralysis, or indeed movement, through hypnotism, is in fact the result of a DREAM we have provoked. The CONTENT of the delirium is of no importance... the proof is that the cause of hysteric's thoughts, can be altered at will!

*Cut back towards where AUGUSTINE is now supine.*

AUGUSTINE: She pricked her finger on the spindle and slept for a hundred years. Till it was time to wake. Till it was time to speak. He kissed her mouth and she knew it was time to speak...

*Lights now switch to a murky light over AUGUSTINE's bed. FREUD is there, a confessional atmosphere. Augustine is struggling to utter, FREUD gently encouraging her, fascinated...*

AUGUSTINE: ... eyes... cat's eyes, green and bright and shiny as topaz. The eyes were following me, watching me, out of the darkness. I screamed out loud. Maman came in. My nose was bleeding. She wiped it with a white rag. She called the doctor. The doctor came and looked at my tongue and my nose and inside my eyes. The doctor said I had become a woman. He said: "You are a woman now, Augustine" and

28

gave me some strips of white cotton to put between my legs. He said "This will happen every month now" and then he said "Avoid water" and left. I hurt. I hurt all over. I hurt under my arms and I hurt between my legs where the rat had been. It felt bruised there. Dry. Sore. I vomited. Maman showed me how to use the rags. But the wound stopped bleeding after a few days, and I haven't needed to use the rags since, so the doctor was wrong... wasn't he?

*FREUD is caught offguard.*

FREUD: Mademoiselle?
AUGUSTINE: Well, I'm not a proper woman... am I? (*Suddenly changing the subject.*) Does he like me?
FREUD: Who, Mademoiselle?
AUGUSTINE: The Professor. Does he like me?
FREUD: Yes... I... Do you want him to like you?
AUGUSTINE: Of course! Well, don't you?
FREUD: I suppose...
AUGUSTINE: And do they like me?
FREUD: They?
AUGUSTINE: The audience...
FREUD: Oh I'm sure they must do... Some of them come to the hospital especially to see you...
AUGUSTINE: Am I famous then?
FREUD: I suppose you could say...
AUGUSTINE: Is he famous?
FREUD: Yes, he is...
AUGUSTINE: More famous than me?
FREUD: Well, yes, he is...
AUGUSTINE: That's not fair!
FREUD: Mademoiselle?
AUGUSTINE: I have to suffer for my art!... Are you famous?
FREUD: Er, no, mademoiselle...
AUGUSTINE: Do you want to be famous, Dr. Freud? Imagine doctors wanting to be famous!

(*She giggles. She is 'playing' FREUD at his own curiosity.*)

AUGUSTINE: Do you like me?

*Freud, taken by surprise, embarrassed, fumbles for his hanky and sneezes. Lights switch to 'amphitheatre'. AUGUSTINE's bed rushed quite violently to center stage. CHARCOT is now using her body as a specimen, touching various parts, under breasts, etc., as he speaks.*

CHARCOT: HYSTEROGENIC POINTS Messieurs! Like secret geysers in the landscape of hysteria! A touch and the attack is cured! The same touch, and the attack is provoked! You will find the location of these... hot spots... invariably under the breasts and on the ovaries of course! Observe!

*He presses AUGUSTINE's ovaries again, this time harder. She starts to scream out, her body convulsing.*

AUGUSTINE: Pig! Pig! You're HURTING ME! Pig! catch the rats, catch the rats! The rats are getting bigger! My throat! Oh my throat hurts... Something pulling my tongue! My throat! What do you know about making me better?... I don't want you anywhere near me!... I won't uncross my legs!... Oh you've hurt me too much... No you won't... Help!... Bastard! Nurd! Lousy jerk! Excuse me! Excuse me, Monsieur, leave me alone!

CHARCOT: *(Gesturing Freud to take her away.)* Doctor!

AUGUSTINE: I'm telling you, get rid of that snake, the one in your trousers! It's bad, bad, bad, bad, bad, bad, (etc.)

*Charcot nods paternally at AUGUSTINE's yells, watching her being wheeled out.*

CHARCOT: See how hysterics scream and shout? Much ado about nothing!

*BLACKOUT leaving only the projection of the photo of AUGUSTINE. THE VIOLINIST appears, like some visiting spirit. She plays a slow piece of music, perhaps Chopin. The curtains draw. AUGUSTINE performs the dance of her contortion and seizure – a slow, perverse pin-up replicating the same original photo which is now projected huge.*

*Throughout, on the other side of the stage, tight head-and-shoulders-light on CHARCOT and FREUD. They take fat cigars, and, like a vaudeville double act, perform in unison the rituals of rolling, licking, snipping and lighting their smoke. They suck furiously and deliciously on them. Augustine slips away.*

CHARCOT: Theory is all very well, Herr Doctor, but some things exist which have nothing to do with preconcieved theory...

FREUD: If only we knew WHAT existed...

CHARCOT: This cigar exists. We exist. Hysteria exists.

FREUD: Herr Professor, you know you were talking of the adventure, the courage to see the new? Well... I, er... have been thinking. Couldn't it all be an antic disposition... a... an outward performance if you like... of some deeper story trying to be told? Of a sexual nature... I have noticed, with Mlle Dubois, whose words during an attack I have been documenting as you asked...

CHARCOT: Herr Freud, I merely asked you to record what occurred, physically and vocally...

FREUD: Quite so, yes. But it is as though she... trusts... me with certain information. As though she wants me to hear... embarassing things, intimate things which she could never say, nor should ever say in, er, normal everyday life. As though I remind her of someone she feels familiar with. A relative, father, or uncle maybe...

CHARCOT: Dr Freud, unorthodox as we are proud to be here, we none the less adhere stringently to the ethics of our profession, namely: it is inappropriate, not to say inadmissible, to develop particular affection for the patients. They will always compete for our attention. Our job is to step back, take a good look, keep our minds clear for our scientific purpose!

FREUD: But of course, Professeur; it's just that Mlle Dubois' body would seem to have become... a theatre for forgotten scenes!...

CHARCOT: Too much Sarah Bernhardt, Herr Doctor, and not enough Salpêtrière, eh?

(*He laughs paternally, FREUD is annoyed at not succeeding to arouse CHARCOT's interest.'*)

You are a fine doctor! An astute neurologist! Who knows, one day you too might achieve some eminence in our tough profession. It needs ambition! And obsession, Herr Doctor! We must think as scientists and not let ourselves be manipulated by the febrile imaginings of young girls!

FREUD: Professeur Charcot, I...

CHARCOT: Dr Freud, I look forward to receiving the results of your comparative study of hysteric and motor paralyses. Very much!... And now, I must leave you. Back to Neuilly before the rain comes down, eh? You must come and have dinner with us. Soon! Fridays at the Charcots are something of an institution!

FREUD: So I've heard from some of the interns!

CHARCOT: My wife and I like to entertain! Talk about something other than shop! Get to meet some interesting people so you can report back home that 'le tout Paris' is alive and kicking, eh!?

FREUD: I'd like that very much, Professor.

CHARCOT: Good, good! Oh what a noble mind is here o'erthrown!

*He taps his finger on FREUD's forehead. He exits, laughing. FREUD stubs his cigar out with his foot. Looks after him. Suddenly remembering:*

FREUD: ... I dreamt... you kissed me three times there... (*indicates forehead where he has just been tapped*)... Herr César!

*BLACKOUT. VIOLINIST starts to play. A lush and lugubrious forest slide washes the set. It is darkish and leafy. Rain is pouring. AUGUSTINE, in her nightgown, turns slowly in a shower of water, as though slaking a huge thirst. The sound of water magnifies. She is singing. Suddenly, lights fade up as AUGUSTINE tumbles on to her bed, as though pushed from behind. We hear on soundtrack a door slam. She weeps, shaking with wet and cold. Lights pass through 'dawn' to 'morning', bright, birdsong. The VIOLINIST stops playing. FREUD enters. As though on his way to somewhere, anxious to avoid contact with her... She catches his eye. He hesitates, pauses...*

AUGUSTINE: Doctor! Doctor, I'm thirsty. I got that sugary taste again...
FREUD: I'll get you some water. (*He pours her some water from a pitcher into a tin mug. Hands it to her. She drinks it in one greedy go. Hands it back.*)
AUGUSTINE: My throat's sore. It's always so sore after amyl nitrate...
FREUD: You prefer cold water treatment?

*AUGUSTINE pretends not to pick up his reference. Starts to brush her hair.*

FREUD: Tell me about your night, mademoiselle. The nurses were worried. It was a terribly wet night and you had next to nothing on...
AUGUSTINE: Will there by any photos today? I must look terrible...
FREUD: Tell me about your night.
AUGUSTINE: (*As if suddenly deciding to trust him a little.*) The night was hot. I thought I was going to suffocate. The air was growling like a cat about to pounce! And then the skies broke and there was lots of loud explosions and this big hot rain came down to wash it all clean... I had to be outside, under the avenue of trees. I wasn't going to run away, you know. I don't want to run away... now... I'm not ready yet...
FREUD: Ready?

*AUGUSTINE's face contorts in disgust. She has just remembered a dream, and she is recalling it.*

FREUD: Fräulein Dubois?
AUGUSTINE: I just remembered my dream... I'm in an abattoir. Inside are lots of pigs, cows, sheep, chickens. I see them kill them. Kill pigs... one by one with big knives... slit them open from their throats to their bottoms... huge wounds... their insides spilling out... them... screaming, trying to run away.... then cut! cut! cut! and they lie there, all big and skin-pink, with such a frightened look in their eyes... and they lie there in pools of blood. Then everything is soaked in blood... the floor, the walls, the men's hands, my dress... all red...
FREUD: Fräulein Dubois?

*She is lost in her own dream images and doesn't respond. Freud moves towards her as if to start examining her. Lights cut. Red slide projection. Or red tint on a black and white one?*

*Lights up on CHARCOT stage right, sitting in an armchair, his 'office', profile to audience. Very engrossed in heavy tones.*

CHARCOT: Come in!

*FREUD enters, excited.*

FREUD: Monsieur le Professeur. Fräulein Dubois has started her menses!
CHARCOT: Fräulein who?
FREUD: Fräulein... Mademoiselle Dubois – Augustine – The one you've been using in public lectures Monsieur le Professeur...
CHARCOT: Ah yes, of course. Our young pearl! Has she had any attacks in the last few days?
FREUD: Yes, Monsieur le Professeur. You remember a couple of weeks ago she was having some bad ones, and you had prescribed the ovarian compressor? Well she had visions then.

*Lights fade up on AUGUSTINE who choruses with FREUD. NB: the extra words indicate AUGUSTINE's version where different from FREUD's. He is animated, excited. She has an expression of staring horror.*

FREUD: She was in a theatre... there was a play about a revolution.
AUGUSTINE: I

Big men with red eyes and blue teeth were shooting each other. A man next to her/me was shot, in the head. He lay next to her/me, bleeding... then, she/I saw cartloads of corpses, pulled by six big black beasts. The corpses were emaciated, lights shone from their eyes, their mouths hung open. They were surrounded by ten men calling to her/me – *Fräulein Dubois* – who was surrounded by flames, big black crows, and a Tricolore flag!

*Lights out on AUGUSTINE.*

Well, these attacks have been continuing on and off this past fortnight and then in the last few days have accelerated. During some of them she also saw huge rats with long tails. Anyway, the concierge found her in the middle of the night under the trees, with nothing on... but her nightgown, sir, and the rain was pouring down. She was soaked through for hours out there. When she was brought back to the ward she was in a state of semi-hallucination. I gave her a small dose of amyl nitrate. Another series of nightmares, this time a slaughterhouse. Blood, lots of red in it. I saw her this morning, examined her, and she's most definitely bleeding!

CHARCOT: So our young Doctor has a keen ear and our young – WOMAN – a vivid imagination!
FREUD: Well, yes, Monsieur le Professeur.
CHARCOT: What did I tell you, eh?!
FREUD: Quite, Monsieur le Professeur.
CHARCOT: Thank you for your report, Dr Freud.

*FREUD visibly doesn't want to leave it there, and awaits his cue.*

CHARCOT: Will that be all, Dr Freud?
FREUD: Well... You see I just wondered, about those dream images, recurring. Just like in her attacks... rats, snakes, eyes, blood... she's always... bringing them up...
CHARCOT: My dear Herr Doctor. The first thing you must learn about our hysterics is that they may have particularly lively minds, excited no doubt by reading cheap novels and romances! Then they come here and spend a lot of time lying on their backs – fiction affliction! Now the disease is precipitated by some trauma no doubt and of course we cannot ignore a predisposition to hysteria, nor its hereditary basis, true. Madness breeds madness! And the past may shape the present! But we won't find the answer in her chattering, Herr Doctor. And certainly not in dreams! No, the answer lies IN THE BODY. We have to think anatomically and physiologically! Hysterics flock to us like so many sphinxes...
FREUD: Well precisely, Professeur. That is just what I'm thinking... Mademoiselle Dubois is like a sphinx! That is a brilliant way of putting it! A sphinx with a riddle...
CHARCOT: Solving that riddle is my life's work, Dr Freud. Hm! Chacun à son clue! Now, I thank you for your report. You have an exceptionally forceful mind. So, Mlle Dubois needs constant recording. Photographs both in the lab and in the ward. We shall continue with gold, morphine and amyl nitrate. Liberal use of ovarian compressor. And regular vaginal swabs. Yes?
FREUD: Yes, of course, but...
CHARCOT: One step at a time, Dr Freud! Fly in the face of the establishment we must if we are to advance at all! But, the answer lies in the BODY, Dr Freud, THE BODY!
FREUD: Monsieur le Professeur, I'm merely interested...
CHARCOT: Now, if you will excuse me...

*Charcot gets up. FREUD passes him his hat, coat, stick, etc. Resigned silence.*

CHARCOT: Been to the theatre lately?
FREUD: Yes, Monsieur le Professeur. The Comédie Française season.
CHARCOT: Sarah Bernhardt?
FREUD: (*Nods*) *Joan of Arc.*
CHARCOT: Ah! The Divine Sarah!
FREUD: She was... mesmerising...
CHARCOT: The Divine Joan! Burnt as a witch! Voices, voices, they all hear voices!

*He exits, in good humour. FREUD concentrates into the middle distance a minute, then leaves, angry and frustrated.*

*Still in blackout, we hear the violinist playing passionately. Lights up on AUGUSTINE lying under her bed. She starts as though hearing a voice. Then singing to herself, she seeks her ribbons from under her pillow, furtive.*

AUGUSTINE: Ach, du liebe Augustine, Augustine, Augustine, ach, du liebe Augustine, alles ist hin... . Oh, my pretty Augustine, Augustine, Augustine... . I like the red ones best and the blue ones second best... . Oh, ma belle Augustine, Augustine Au...

*Lights suddenly bleach out the colours of the ribbons. She screams, her gaze transfixed in horror on a ribbon she has been tying. The violinist picks up the pitch of her scream and continues to play that note on vibrato throughout the following:*

AUGUSTINE: It's all gone! It's all gone! All the colour's gone! Maman! No, no, no! I can't see my colours! It's all gone grey! Help, someone HELP!! HELP ME!!! I CAN'T SEE MY COLOURS! THEY'VE TAKEN MY COLOURS AWAY!

*She is frantically running round her bed, crying, screaming and rattling the iron frame.*
BLACKOUT.

*Lights up on VIOLINIST in a tight overhead light. She shifts the vibrato note into painful, high-pitched playing.*

*Lights snap to AUGUSTINE, struggling against the two men with their backs to the audience, their arms locked in hers, pulling her backwards. Her eyes are fixed in rage and fright on someone in the audience. She spits.*

AUGUSTINE: How dare you! How dare you come to the Salpêtrière! Who let you in? I'll tell on you! Whoever let you in is a shit!... A man like you! A respectable middle-aged man! A family man!! With a housekeeper for a whore! What do you want with her daughter, eh?! I bet Maman doesn't know you're here!... I hate you! I see your eyes, shining like topazes! Well they can't get me anymore, not here!... I'm going to tell on you... . If only they'd LISTEN!!! I decided Sunday before last... in church... I prayed to Saint Theresa that you would die! Bastard! Bastard! Pig! Get rid of that snake in your trousers! I don't want a rat in my bctto... MAMAN!!... I don't want doctors' fingers! I don't want measurements! I don't want pictures! I don't want performances! I don't want amyl nitrate!!!

*She screams, weeps, struggles. BLACKOUT. Violin continues playing.*

*When lights come up again AUGUSTINE is on the bed (now stripped of its bows) in a sour beam of light making patterns of prison bars. A cold, uncomfortable atmosphere. She has been locked up. She is holding her arms out in a supplicatory pose. There is a camera flash. She relaxes. Adjusts her clothing. Lights discover FREUD, as though the director of the photosession. He scribbles something on a pad. Picks up a folder.*

AUGUSTINE: Show me!
FREUD: Fräulein?
AUGUSTINE: Pictures
FREUD: Ah! Well they take a long time to change into pictures you can see. You need a darkened room... chemicals...
AUGUSTINE: But this is a darkened room!
FREUD: No, Mademoiselle Dubois, you don't quite understand you see, it...
AUGUSTINE: Are they better than the sketches they've done of me?
FREUD: Well... er, they're more, how shall I say, lifelike...
AUGUSTINE: I want to see them!
FREUD: Mademoiselle Dubois, it takes time, many hours, as I said.
AUGUSTINE: Show me some from another time, some that are already done! What you've got there under your arm.
FREUD: Mademoiselle, Monsieur le Professeur doesn't like patients to see their own pictures unless he...
AUGUSTINE: And if I promise to tell you my dream?...

*AUGUSTINE has caught his eye. FREUD is 'seduced'.*

FREUD: You musn't tell anyone I showed you, promise?
AUGUSTINE: Cross my heart and hope to die!

*FREUD opens a folder he is carrying and selects a few photos for her to look at. She laughs and gasps at them as though they were holiday snaps.*

AUGUSTINE: Is that me? I don't look like that!!
FREUD: They say the camera doesn't lie, Mademoiselle.
AUGUSTINE: People do. Their eyes do. Is this how you see me? Is this one really like me?
FREUD: Mademoiselle, this is how you are, were, for some minutes, holding still until it flashed and recorded your actions... it's a... a... portrait of you... er... having an attack, it's...
AUGUSTINE: But I look so... MESSY!...

*(She glances closer at one of the pictures and frowns in anger)*

But what's this? (*FREUD looks at the pictures as she runs through them, reading from them.*) 'Amorous Supplication'! 'Eroticism'! 'Ecstasy'! Who gave them titles? How does he know? He doesn't understand a thing! He never listens! He doesn't know anything! What does he know? Professor Prod, Professor Prick! You know what Herr Doctor? You know what I think? I think he's got a real nerve! But... if he thinks I'm being good I'll get more shows, and if I get more shows, well... it's better...
FREUD: Better?
AUGUSTINE: Of course.
FREUD: Because you like the public lectures?
AUGUSTINE: Because so long as he needs me he'll let me out of here, let me back in the ward. I can't stand it in here, Doctor. I don't like bars on the windows. I don't like these soft walls. It's no way to treat... a star!

*BLACKOUT. VIOLINIST plays*

*Lights cross-fade to find a tableau of CHARCOT addressing an audience at a Tuesday Lesson. Freud is supporting AUGUSTINE, who is standing weeping, from behind as in Une Leon Clinique de Charcot (the painting by Brouillet). A beam of light shines directly onto AUGUSTINE's bosom. Her gown falls off her shoulders. Applause is heard and the tableau comes alive.*

CHARCOT: Gentlemen. Our patient has lately maintained a pattern of an average of 200 attacks a week. Ether has proved unsuccessful in abating them, whereas she responds exceptionally well to amyl nitrate. The ovarian compressor (*he holds the metal contraption up for the audience to see*) has also been used to suppress attacks with some success. She has had fits of rage, provoked by the smallest annoyance. Following one of these she was found yet again, barefoot, in her nightgown, outdoors in the gardens in torrential rain. We had to put her in a straitjacket which she tore. Her extreme unmanageability has obliged us to confine her to a padded cell. So you see the extraordinary energy we are dealing with! An energy you will, shortly I hope, see at work in a full cycle of Grande Hystérie. How, an interesting new development: our patient, upon examination, showed colour blindness, matched by an increase of visual acuity. So, whilst she can only see things in black and white, she is actually seeing more clearly.

*AUGUSTINE suddenly fixes her gaze on someone in the audience, a horrified expression on her face. Screams.*

AUGUSTINE: OH NO! Monsieur Carnot! Not you again!

*She is furious. Her bed is rolled on and she is laid down on it, protesting.*

CHARCOT: Now I want you to appreciate especially the unfolding of the attack. Most important: the spectacle is a single event that unrolls sequentially. Beginning, middle and end. With a climax, and catharsis. Just like a classic play. Or symphony rather. I'm talking about the archetypal model of course. It is most important to learn to identify the archetype. Then you have a yardstick to measure by. So, we will just use a little hysterogenic point to provoke an attack as a form of therapy!

*He presses lightly under her breast. AUGUSTINE arches her back. Her whole body goes rigid. She starts to utter strangled cries. She remains in this arched rigid state whilst CHARCOT speaks.*

CHARCOT: There! Our young lady is entering the prologue of her attack – what we call the 'aura' – which will presently lead into the first movement – the 'epileptoid phase'...
AUGUSTINE: I... can hardly... breathe... I... won't... be... ill... so... as... not... to... have... to... have... any... amyl nitrate!
CHARCOT: You know, when I first came to the Salpêtrière 20 years ago and witnessed these hysterical attacks, I said to myself, "how can it be that such events are not described in the textbooks? How should I go about describing these... displays... from my first hand experience? Hysterics simply befuddled me and I felt irritatingly powerless before them. Then one day, I was struck by a sort of intuition. I said to myself, "Something about them makes them all the same... there is a lowest common denominator which is..."

*He breaks off as AUGUSTINE begins her thrashing.*

CHARCOT: Ah! Now you can see the arched back has become rather pronounced...

AUGUSTINE: Dirty... beast... Pig! Pig! I'll tell Papa! You're so heavy! You're HURTING ME! Kill the rats! Kill the Rats! I don't want a rat in my botto... Mama!... My neck... My neck... I'll go as soon as I can! You're making me a prossie! Put that snake back in your trousers!

*She opens her mouth and puts her hand in as if to take something out. She holds the invisible thing on the palm of her hand and spits on it.*

AUGUSTINE: He dares again! He's got a nerve! Watch out! Watch OUT! You dare come to the Salpêtrière? You DARE come to the Salpêtrière?... the next time you come... you lousy bastard... you are a bad man... you are a very, very bad man!... and you are a disgusting mother! And my father forgave you? If hitting one's mother were allowed, then I'd hit you! I would! How could you go with him! He's a dirty pig, a PIG do you hear! You don't want me to tell the truth! You say I am ruining the family, the household! And I'm telling you, you're not my mother anymore! Don't send me rats! Don't send me your stinking rats!!

CHARCOT: ... and the phase of emotional outbursts... remember the sequence...

CHARCOT: First phase, what we call epileptoid – arched back then vocalizations, then contractures...

*AUGUSTINE is convulsing, arching, twisting.*

CHARCOT: You know, the extraordinary thing about these attacks is that the patient curiously recovers without being in the least bit tired or spent...

*AUGUSTINE suddenly pauses. Sits up. Ties a ribbon on her corsage, adjusts her hair. Resumes fit. CHARCOT doesn't seem surprised.*

CHARCOT: So, now let's use a hysterogenic point again, this time the ovary... here we go again!

*He presses again on her ovary. AUGUSTINE goes into a freeze.*

AUGUSTINE: Maman! I'm scared! Oh, no! Oh, please no! Oh, please don't!

CHARCOT: Note the emotional outburst again.

*AUGUSTINE starts to move into wild and impossible positions, convulsing and arching as before. Each position she arrives at she holds for a beat or two, holding her breath and then releasing out of it into the next phase of contortions.*

CHARCOT: And now we are in the second phase, that we call 'exotic movements' or 'clowning'... as you can see, this... dance... has as its recurring leitmotif, the arched back position, which we call 'arc en cercle'... And I bet some of you are wondering "how is it humanly possible she can do that?" Well, the truth of the matter is, none of us knows where this demonic energy comes from. Makes the Folies Bergères look like a funeral march, eh?!

*He tuts and marvels at AUGUSTINE's extraordinary, agonising, dance. Suddenly she strikes a very stiffened version of one of her 'attitudes passionnelles' poses. We notice the difference because she appears to notice us, the audience, and now be performing for us instead of before us.*

*A slide fades in. It is one of the real AUGUSTINE in identical pose. It drenches the set. The VIOLINIST appears and plays a short vibrato on a high note. The slide fades with the music as the pose releases in tension, softens. Her face lights up with apparent pleasure, then suddenly anger. During the following phase of the attack, AUGUSTINE sometimes addresses the audience directly, sometimes an imaginary man very near to her, sometimes on her bed. She acts it all out. A very cinematic interlude.*

CHARCOT: Ah! Attitudes passionnelles!
AUGUSTINE: You're being silly!... You're making me blush!... Me, crazy?... Oh, now listen!... is it for real or are you teasing me?... You're tickling me! (*She giggles long and loud. Suddenly she stops.*) What? You refuse to believe I'd be faithful? Ah, now come on, now!... That's not fair... we're in the meadow... you try to kiss me. I like it. But I don't like you treating me like I was easy. Then I turn your face around in my hands and I look in your face and suddenly you kiss me. You put your tongue in my mouth. I like it. I like you, I like your smell. Then... suddenly... I remember him! Stop! Vomit!

*Her face contorts in disgust and then fright. She scuttles to the upstage corner of the bed and starts to play out the aggressor and herself with her hands. One hand moves towards her body, the other pulling it away, etc.*

AUGUSTINE: You're so heavy! You're HURTING ME! Put that snake back in your trousers! Oh, the peacocks, the peacocks with their big tails cluttered with eyes! Get your rat out of my botto... Maman! Oh, the pig! The pig!... No, I didn't know that's how babies were made... it made me cry then... I don't think it's all that nice, you know... It's true

I still can't get that big fat pig out of my mind... Oh, please, please!! I beg you to get rid of him! He's got a 22-year-old daughter! A proper gent! When the thing happened, he deserved prison, he did! But I didn't tell! I didn't tell because of my reputation! And because of the knife! I told you about the knife! You what?... Oh, really? And what if I became pregnant here at the Salpêtrière, eh? And had a baby here? What would the doctors say? Oh, we never kiss doctors! Never! Never! Never! Never!... Not even the kind ones.

*She freezes on a particularily exctatic pose, arms outstretched as though reaching for someone above her. The slide and VIOLINIST as before, very brief, then out.*

CHARCOT: Perfect! Which brings us swiftly to the fourth and final phase, a period of delirium.

*AUGUSTINE starts to move more energetically again. She performs some extraordinary rocking movements, her legs tossed above her head, as well as twists and turns as before.*

AUGUSTINE: I won't uncross my legs! NO! You've got a snake too! What do you mean, you won't take no for an... I can't, you hear, can't!... Because I don't like it... no, whatever they say. No rats in my tummy... Oh, so I'm a woman of the world am I? Who says? What do I know? I haven't got time! I haven't got time! I HAVEN'T GOT TIME! Madame is here... I'm telling you that Monsieur is out on business... (*She gazes in space, eyes wide open, smiles, then cries*). I'm telling you, Monsieur Carnot has gone out... Yes, the one who wants my bottom... He'd be furious... I'm telling you I can't... It's impossible... I was going to tell... but Monsieur Carnot said he'd kill me... he had a knife... the way he looked at me to stop me telling... I didn't know what he meant when he showed me... He forced my legs... I didn't know it was a beast that was going to bite me! I want to go out every night, because he wants to get in my bed, when Madame is asleep... He told me outright he'd kill me... I'm telling you, it's him who wanted it... He hurts me. He makes me dry, sore, bloody... he tells me that later it'll do me good... But it's a sin... it's bad, bad, bad... I'll have to leave, you know... I hate him, I really hate him, but I love you, but I can't do that, please, no! Please listen to me!...

CHARCOT: At this point the cycle may commence all over again and may continue for some days. Our patient, during an active period, may have several such attacks in one hour. We may now use the hysterogenic point to alleviate the attack if we so wish.

*He indicates to FREUD to press hard on her ovary. Her attack abates.*

41

CHARCOT: The demon has entered, the demon has left... for the time being. Our patient will rest. She will awake smiling, like Sleeping Beauty from a long absence. She will probably have forgotten all the obscenity she has uttered here in this 'lascivious choreography'. She will, in short, be charm itself.

*Lights snap to violinist stamping out a wild tarantella on Charcot's desktop. Augustine is frantically knotting and tying her bedlinen into huge, futile attempts at escape. She collapses, exhausted on her bed, emptied of emotion. The violinist exits.*

*FREUD enters to find AUGUSTINE, desolate, hugging her knees, rocking, on her bed. She stares out to the audience.*

FREUD: Fräulein Dubois...
AUGUSTINE: Where do colours go when they go?
FREUD: Mademoiselle Dubois...

*AUGUSTINE suddenly relaxes, opens out, smiles and looks at FREUD.*

AUGUSTINE: Doctor! Do sit down! How was I?

*FREUD gingerly sits on the corner of her bed.*

AUGUSTINE: Make me born again!

*Freud places his hands on her head, to hypnotise her, gauche. A healing gesture, but deliberately ambiguous. Blackout.*

*Lights up on AUGUSTINE sitting on the edge of her bed. FREUD is sitting on a chair, taking notes.*

AUGUSTINE: I dreamt I wasn't at the Salpêtrière any longer. I was walking in the Bois de Boulogne. The bluebells were out. I was knee-deep in a lavender sea of them. My skirt was stained by their ink and my boots were wet. Suddenly I heard a flock of starlings and looked up. The tree was peppered with them. They sounded like a million screeching bells. Then, as if by magic, they all stopped singing at once and took flight, wheeling out of sight... out of sight.

*Lights fade to CHARCOT's 'study' area. CHARCOT in profile to audience at his desk, as in previous scene. It is evening. He is working by a small gas lamp. He is smoking a pipe, hugely enjoying it. He is in fact 'high' from his smoke, sketching. A knock at the door.*

CHARCOT: Come in! If you must!

*FREUD enters, sniffs the air, perplexed.*

FREUD:  Ah, Monsieur le Professeur... I've just been sent an article from...
CHARCOT: Welcome to The Club des Assassins, Herr Doctor!
FREUD:  Monsieur le Professeur?
CHARCOT: Assassins! HASHISHIENS! HASH ISH CHIENS!

*He giggles, holds up his sketch for FREUD to see.*

CHARCOT: I wanted to see what all the fuss was about!
FREUD:  The fuss, Monsieur le Professeur?
CHARCOT: Baudelaire, De Nerval. All that lot... *Les Fleurs du Mal*... the artist's nostalgia for mud, the temptation of another state of consciousness... I had to try it for myself... and what I find is I have drawn lots of... bodies and beasts, all co-mingled like some ghastly gothic dream! Definitely... no plan... nothing I wished to convey... just what tumbled out of my mind's eye... see!

*A slide drenches the whole set with Charcot's doodle.*

FREUD:  It's, er, very good, Monsieur le Professeur...
CHARCOT: Good? Rubbish! It's a DOODLE, Herr Doctor, a mere doodle... No compliments, please! I want your powers of analysis!
FREUD:  You want me to tell you what I think?
CHARCOT: Why, yes!

*Freud wanders around the images, dwarfed by mutant beasts, genitals, etc., curious, unsure of what to do.*

FREUD:  Well, it's er...
CHARCOT: Yes?
FREUD:  It's... erotic... Monsieur le Professeur!
CHARCOT: I might have guessed! (*Pauses.*) I suppose it is rather, when you look at it like that... ha, ha... it always comes down to genitals in the end...
FREUD:  But I thought you didn't...
CHARCOT: "Don't think," my mother always used to say, "leave it to the horses. They've got a bigger head than you!"

*Great mirth ensues from Charcot and Freud is baffled.*

FREUD:  Monsieur le Professeur, now maybe isn't the time...

CHARCOT: Herr Doctor, my mind is as clear as a bell. Just... exceptional lucidity... I'm all ears... (*giggles*) I'm all ears!!!

FREUD: Monsieur le Professeur... I have just been sent an article from Vienna about a most interesting case there... a young hysteric... a case presenting a variegated picture of paralysis and contractures, inhibitions and states of mental confusion.

CHARCOT: So, as I always say, we do not invent hysteria here, eh?!

FREUD: No, Monsieur le Professeur. The thing is this: a chance observation showed her physician that she could be relieved of these clouded states of consciousness if she was induced by hypnosis to express in words the affective fantasy by which she was at that moment dominated...

CHARCOT: Ah! But amyl nitrate makes our young ladies most loquacious. And you yourself have made copious notes of Mlle Dubois, as I recall. No, there is nothing stopping the flow of words in this hospital... the corridors are positively cacophanous!

FREUD: No, but... it's about listening to the meaning... to what they say. That's the point he's findi...

CHARCOT: (*Standing up.*) I listen with my eyes, Herr Doctor... That's the difference between us... veni, vidi, vici!!!

*He roars with laughter, nods for FREUD to pass him his hat, coat and stick.*

CHARCOT: All female hysterics cry rape! Fantasy, Herr Doctor! We are an audience for their obscene imaginings! Now, if you'll excuse me, I didn't realise it was so late... lost track of time. My wife is most keen to meet the Young Turk from Vienna! Next Friday it is, eh! she LOVES to talk, so if you're a good listener...

*He sweeps out, singing 'La Donna è Mobile', his sketch under his arm.*

*FREUD is left half pleased, half insulted, certainly stunned by the meeting. He sniffs the air, smiles, take out a cigar. The moment he lights it, the VIOLINIST starts to play.*

*Lights change so that he is still in the same position, smoking, but is now in the same space as AUGUSTINE, who is sitting on the bed. She is clutching a handful of neutral coloured ribbons. She is twisting her hands in them. FREUD moves to the head of her bed, detatched, interrogating, he is becoming a Freudian...*

FREUD: You were saying...
AUGUSTINE: I forget...

FREUD: Your feelings for Monsieur Carnot... these were... these were... uncomfortable, perhaps... nice feelings, but... uncomfortable perhaps?

AUGUSTINE: I didn't say that!!

FREUD: Tell me about Monsieur Carnot, Mademoiselle Dubois, the first thing which springs to mind.

AUGUSTINE: He smoked cigars. You can never get rid of... the smell... the way his breath smells... (*Darkening.*) Once I passed him on the stairs... I was on my way to the kitchen... my arms were full of bread. I'd just come from the bakery. I turned away so as not to have to look into his eyes... he pulled my hair and made me look in his face. He said I was a filthy whore and he'd kill me if I told anyone... Then he said: "What's for dinner?". And I said: "Pig's liver". (*Suddenly crying.*) I did it because I was frightened! Have you ever been frightened, Doctor?

*She suspends, lost in the recall.*

FREUD: So you think he was really saying he'd kill you, Monsieur Carnot?

AUGUSTINE: (*Angry.*) I don't think, I know! He did!... That night at dinner, my mother and I were serving table. I wanted to tell. I wanted to shout out to my mother, I wanted to tell her he'd done it. I wanted to tear his hair out for being so disgusting!

FREUD: So... you wanted your mother to play a part in your relationship with Monsieur Carnot?...

AUGUSTINE: I wanted to throw soup in her face because I'm sure she knew and she wouldn't say it! And because she had known him. He had touched her and she had liked it...

FREUD: What kind of feelings do you get when you think of your mother and Monsieur Carnot?

AUGUSTINE: He caught my eyes in his gaze. They were terrible. Green. Bright. Like topaz. They said: "If you ever tell I'll kill you!"

FREUD: So why do you feel you want to tell me this story?

*She doesn't look at FREUD who is looking at her with deep concentration, still smoking. She is in considerable distress. Anguished at Freud's pressure.*

*The VIOLINIST plays. AUGUSTINE curls up in her bed and pulls the sheets over her. FREUD stubs out his cigar. Moves downstage. Meticulously prepares some cocaine, evidently nervous. He sniffs it with all the greed of an addict. He is facing out to the audience. A soundtrack fades up as he performs this ritual. Clinking of glasses and cutlery, laughter, male and female:*

CHARCOT: *Of course I'm zoophile! That's why there's a sign above my door at the hospital: No Dog Laboratories Here! I hate bloodsports with a passion.*

*What can be more barbaric than hunting? It is man's festival of murder! The only huntress I can accept is Diana! Naked, her bow in her hand, arrows in her quiver, running through the forest barefoot, caring not a jot, neither for her outfit nor the danger. No, one thing I can't stand in the country today is the sight of these velvet-clad lady-huntresses of ours, pistol in hand, ready to shoot the nearest pigeon. It is utterly revolting!*

*Sounds of much laughter.*

MALE VOICE: *Perhaps, Professor, Diana's nudity may have something to do with the exception you make for her!*

CHARCOT: *Why certainly, I find her pleasing! She's Nature herself, the personification of its forces, a symbol...*

*We hear a doorbell ring. Freud's face, out to audience, literally lights up to greet his hosts, he raises his hat, offers his hand.*

CHARCOT: *Ah! Why, welcome, Dr. Freud! We were just discussing the ethics concerning the meat on our plates!*

*The stage is suddenly flooded with the slide projection of the trees and greenery as before. Sounds of dinner party merriment, FREUD's voice joining in the laughter. This merging with sounds of heavy rain smatterings of the dinner party blowing in and out. The VIOLINIST live and visible, perhaps on the bed. AUGUSTINE in her 'slice of nature', is turning, catching raindrops on her tongue. Then hugs herself and rocks. She is talking to the trees.*

AUGUSTINE: I love you trees! I love you! You are all right side up! I'm all upside down! Yes, I'm an upside down festival! I'm the impossible dance! I'm the sabbath! I'm the spider dance! I'm a Tarantella! Look at me dance! I've been asleep for a hundred years! A hundred years! I'm a Walpurgis night! I am bad smells, wicked, terrible bad smells! I'm sour milk. I'm a feast of roses. I'm pot-pourri. I'm bad blood. I curdle mayonnaise!! I'm tears and snot and the wet from inside!! I'm the flood! Press it out! Press it our of me! I'm sour grapes! Trample me and you'll get wine! Sour wine, mind, wine to rot your guts! Press it out of me! Press my soul out of me! I want to be born all over again! I'm so angry! I'm so angry! I! Where am I to stand? I look for myself and don't see myself in any of it! I'm a volcano! You'd better watch out! I will pour hot lava all over your cities and your hospitals! I will burn them up! I am a gun! I will shoot, bang, bang, bang! I'm a bird. I'm a snake. I'm a bird and a snake. I slither and I peck and I eat eggs whole and I fly! I'm spit! I'm juices! I'm lots of crying! Listen trees, listen, will you! I'm a bad, bad, bad, bad...

*She throws herself on her bed as before (i.e. as though pushed from behind) as slide cuts and soundtrack quietens. We are back in the ward.*

AUGUSTINE: I've been asleep for a hundred years. It's time to wake. Time to speak...

*She curls up on the bed and pulls the sheets over her head. A light brings FREUD into the scene. We are 'in the middle' of something.*

FREUD: Try to remember. You were alone with Monsieur Carnot.
AUGUSTINE: No! I can't... I want to remember everything. As it was. When Professeur Charcot puts me to sleep, I can't remember anything... I can't even remember my dreams...

*She sleeps. Now CHARCOT joins FREUD to peer at her in the gloomy light.*

FREUD: She has been like this for 22 hours, Monsieur le Professeur.
CHARCOT: How can this be?
FREUD: Well... Monsieur le Professeur...er... when you hypnotised her yesterday... you... you inadvertently forgot to bring her round at the end... Monsieur...
CHARCOT: Is that so? My! my! So we have here a case of an attack of artificial sleep... fascinating!

*He peels back the sheet. He touches her breast. She screams, convulses and utters.*

AUGUSTINE: Pig! Pig! I'll tell! I will. I'll tell! Maman! I can't breathe! There's a lump in my throat and it's getting bigger! Oh, please help me! I'm suffocating! I can't breathe... I...

*CHARCOT nods to FREUD. They hold her still.*

CHARCOT: Amyl Nitrate.

*CHARCOT takes a bottle from FREUD and makes her inhale through a handkerchief. She calms down.*

FREUD: Tell me, Augustine, what happens to you when we make you sleep?
AUGUSTINE: You imagine you've been dreaming, but in fact you've just been hearing people talk.
CHARCOT: (*Suddenly interested.*) What else?
AUGUSTINE: I go upside down.

CHARCOT: Upside down?
AUGUSTINE: I think I love you when really I hate you.

*BLACKOUT. The VIOLINIST plays an eerie cylical waltz. Music continues throughout the following tableaux, which should have the effect of a silent movie.*

*AUGUSTINE has her tongue stuck out very far and rigid. CHARCOT is pointing to it with a baton.*

*BLACKOUT.*

*A flashgun is exploded and we see AUGUSTINE in a frozen pose of shock.*

*BLACKOUT.*

*CHARCOT puts her fingers to AUGUSTINE's lips and we see her blow us lots of kisses.*

*BLACKOUT.*

*AUGUSTINE is lying, rigid, in catalepsy, across two chair backs. CHARCOT is stacking huge gold coins on her.*

*BLACKOUT.*

*AUGUSTINE waltzes, with an imaginary partner, encouraged by CHARCOT as FREUD watches.*

*AUGUSTINE is made to kneel. She takes up a praying position as before. Music stops.*

CHARCOT: What do you see?
AUGUSTINE: God
CHARCOT: What else do you see?
AUGUSTINE: Jesus.
CHARCOT: Alone?
AUGUSTINE: No, why, there's hundreds of them! I thought there was only one little Jesus!
CHARCOT: Anything else?
AUGUSTINE: The Virgin Mary.
CHARCOT: What does she look like?
AUGUSTINE: She has her hands in prayer... there's a rainbow above her head... and a beautiful light behind her... pinkish... white...
CHARCOT: And?

AUGUSTINE: She's stepping on a snake that's at her feet...
CHARCOT: Anything else you'd like to tell the audience?
AUGUSTINE: She's talking to Magdalena!... AND SHE'S LAUGHING!!!

*With increasing speed and frenzy, a montage of photographs – close-ups, etc. – flash around the stage so that the effect is almost stroboscopic. The audience's eye is giddied. VIOLINIST plays, her white gown picking up the projections as she darts about the stage. A cacophanous crescendo of sound like a whirlpool into which all the sounds of her story concentrate.*

*Drumrolls. AUGUSTINE bursts on stage, bringing warm, rich coloured lighting with her, as though the stage had suddenly switched from black and white to technicolor. Dressed in a mixture of CHARCOT's and FREUD's clothes, including top hat and cane, she is a strange, battered, vaudeville drag artiste. FREUD and CHARCOT are sitting on chairs. They are both in shirtsleeves and long johns. Defrocked, they look vulnerable, like babies. They stare out like statues.*

AUGUSTINE: My Doctors, sirs, messieurs! No more emotion pictures! No more secretions for you! No more exhibition! No more stories! I'm leaving your stage! The masterpiece has been stolen! Writing remains. Words fly off... You will see my body fly away into a thousand sparks. I will fly away. My crisis will shatter into millions of crystal splinters, like stars pricking the sky. I will disappear. Dis-membered. I will return. Re-membered. I will come together again in a form you won't recognise. Me and my magical body! I will be immortal. I will be salt. I will parch your mouths dry. Then I will tell everything, as I remembered myself. And you, you will put your tools down, you will listen, really listen, and you will believe every word I say...

*She turns and leaves the stage by a window of light, as though performing a conjuring trick. The VIOLINIST plays the tune of "Ach, du liebe Augustine" as the sound of a heavy, purgative rainfall breaks. The two men, sitting in their underwear, look impassively at the audience.*

*A very very slow fade on the two men.*
*BLACKOUT.*

**THE END**

**Other titles in the Contemporary Theatre Studies series:**